PARANORMAL
ESSEX

PARANORMAL
ESSEX

DAVID SCANLAN & PAUL ROBINS

AMBERLEY

This book is dedicated to:

Sharon Thornton (1970–2012) – A friend, companion and investigator with the Hampshire Ghost Club for many years. Courageous and strong to the end.

John Rayner (1969–2010) – Ghosthunter and inspiration to all who knew him.

First published 2012

Amberley Publishing
The Hill, Stroud
Gloucestershire, GL5 4EP

www.amberley-books.com

British Library Cataloguing in Publication Data.
A catalogue record for this book is available from the British Library.

ISBN 978 1 84868 460 7

Typeset in 10pt on 12pt Sabon.
Typesetting and Origination by Amberley Publishing.
Printed in the UK.

Contents

Acknowledgements 7

Introduction 8

How to Use this Book 9

Ghost Hunting: An Introduction 10

Ambresbury Banks, Epping Forest 15

Angel Public House, Braintree 16

Beam Valley Country Park, Dagenham 17

Beeleigh Abbey, Maldon 18

Benfleet Conservative Club, Benfleet 19

Borley Rectory, Braintree 20

Canvey Island 24

Champions Hall, South Woodham Ferrers 25

Coachman Inn, Earls Colne 27

Coalhouse Fort, East Tilbury 29

Colchester Castle, Colchester 35

Cross Keys Hotel, Saffron Walden 38

Garrison Arms, Shoeburyness 40

Grays Beach, Thurrock 43

Great Chalvedon Hall, Pitsea 45

Hadleigh Castle, Hadleigh 47

Hangman's Hill, High Beech 50

Harwich Redoubt, Harwich 51

Kelvedon Hatch Nuclear Bunker, Braintree 53

Lagenhoe Church, Colchester 58

Little Walden, Uttlesford 62

Maltings, Saffron Walden 63

Matthew Hopkins, Various Parts of Essex 65

Mersea Island Causeway, Mersea Island   69
Moot Hall, Maldon   70
Old Tilbury Fire Station, Tilbury   71
Palace Theatre, Westcliff-On-Sea   72
Priory Park, Southend-On-Sea   74
Purdeys Estate, Rochford   77
Red Lion Hotel, Colchester   81
Rochford Hall, Rochford   87
Saffron Walden, Uttlesford   88
Southend Pier, Southend-On-Sea   89
St James the Less, Hadleigh   93
St Nicholas' Church, Canewdon   95
St Osyth Priory, St Osyth   99
Sun Inn, Saffron Walden   100
Swan Hotel, Brentwood   101
Valentines Mansion, Ilford   103
Walton Hall Museum, Stanford-Le-Hope   105
Bibliography   107
About the Author: David Scanlan   108
About the Author: Paul Robins   109

Acknowledgements

No book can ever be written without calling upon the immense wealth of knowledge held by local people. Therefore the authors would like to extend their thanks and appreciation to Sheila Norton-Badrul, Ghost Hunt Team – team members Colin Smith, Liz Smith, Andrew Ball, Chris Weet and Denise Smith, Thanet Paranormal Investigations – team members Joan Furman and Katy Tearle, Coral Wood, Steve Moyle of Ghost Hunt Events, Brook Hotels, Warren Browning, Walton Hall Museum and Ben Street. Thanks to Jake Flood for his wonderful introduction to this book. Sincere thanks to Peter Underwood for his feedback on the Borley Rectory case. Of course there are also many others to thank and if your name has not appeared here please accept our apologies but duly recognise that without your input this book would not have been possible.

Introduction

Every mile I eat up on the motorways, through the night into the dawn, I am wide-eyed, full of questions and thirsty for more knowledge, knowing that in just a few more hours it's back to the day job.

A team leader and investigator with the Hampshire Ghost Club, I have had the privilege of investigating historical buildings, land and private residencies, leading a team of like-minded paranormal enthusiasts from different backgrounds to gather scientifically measurable evidence through traditional and modern investigation techniques. On many occasions we have captured compelling evidence of the existence of ghosts, yet still we receive plenty of opposition from the sceptics. We also uncover many rational explanations of reported ghostly activity, thus gaining a clearer understanding of the differences between natural phenomena and the paranormal.

As I sit in the glow of the monitor, preparing this Introduction, I also have the latest investigation report open in front of me. I put together the evidence and the events of the years and centuries before my existence come into focus, for investigating the paranormal is as much a journey into history as it is into the unknown.

The lives and practices of the past generations of human life unravel before me; the tragedies, scandals, mysteries and the nature of life and death are remembered. History is brought to life once more through fascinating true ghost stories!

In the pages of *Paranormal Essex* you will find stories to enthral and intrigue, stories that will make you consider the possibility that there really is an afterlife. The authors have selected a wide range of stories from across Essex, sifting the wheat from the chaff to bring you the very best stories from this most haunted of counties.

The truth is out there. Maybe you will find the evidence for yourself, armed with good investigation techniques and, of course, *Paranormal Essex*.

Jake Flood
Team leader and investigator – Hampshire Ghost Club

How to Use this Book

This book has been designed to give you the easiest and most enjoyable reading format possible. Therefore it was apparent from an early stage that the best possible layout for *Paranormal Essex* was an easy to follow A to Z guide format. This means that finding the story you are particularly interested in is simple and it allows you to pick up and put down the book as required; this is particularly useful when researching specific locations but also aids in reading the book cover to cover.

As an extra addition to *Paranormal Essex* we have also included a very brief guide to getting started in ghost hunting. This guide has been completely revised and updated specifically for this book.

Ghost Hunting:
An Introduction

One of the most common questions I am asked by people wanting to conduct their own ghost hunt is 'Where do I begin?'.

In this brief introduction I hope to cover some of the basics. Many would-be paranormal enthusiasts out there are under the impression that in order to investigate your own hauntings you need lots of expensive equipment that can take years to acquire, and although this is true in order to conduct in-depth research, there are some basics that will help you in your quest for evidence of the paranormal.

Your first stop should be to compile an account of what has actually been occurring at your chosen haunted venue. Have there been sightings, disembodied voices, objects mysteriously moving around or sudden increases in temperature? These are all things that you would want to take into consideration. If a ghost has been spotted by someone at the property then try to get this witness account first-hand. Interview the person, if possible, as this will ultimately reveal the finer details of the encounter.

Once your background information on what has been experienced has been collected and organised you can then look into the history of the building and make notes of anything you consider that could be relevant. Was there a tragic death on the premises? Was there a long period of occupation by a particular resident that could explain a ghost reluctant to leave? Are they emotionally bonded to the venue?

Ensure your background research is as in-depth and thorough as it can possibly be. All of this information will help you at a later date and only when you have your dossier and a good working knowledge of your haunted location can your hunt begin.

When we discuss paranormal investigation equipment many people instantly rush into buying high-specification digital cameras or night vision camcorders (many companies have discontinued these in recent years), but remember, one of the best pieces of equipment you can have is yourself, for you could be the next witness to the ghostly apparition you are investigating and your personal experience of the encounter will linger with you for years to come. Many pieces of 'evidence' captured by paranormal investigators fail to stand up to the rigours of scientific scrutiny but if you are the witness and you know that you have tried to explain your encounter in every possible way then you will know for sure that you truly have had an encounter with the paranormal. An accurate and reliable witness statement is just as valuable as any paranormal photograph or electronic voice recording!

Equipment is obviously important though and you should purchase the best equipment possible within your price range. Also, don't forget some very basic and essential items. Here is brief list of equipment the amateur ghost hunter will want to acquire:

Notepads and pens
Clipboard
Voice recorder (digital preferred)
Digital camera (try to avoid cameras with a low mega pixel rating)
Camcorder and plenty of spare tapes or discs
A torch and spare batteries.

Notepads and pens are important for recording essential information, such as the times of experiences and also at what times certain experiments were established. Remember to take plenty of pens as they have the habit of running out at the most inconvenient times!

A clipboard is equally invaluable. In many haunted places it is very common not to be able find a flat, level surface in order to make your notes or draw maps and diagrams, this is especially so in graveyards and other external locations.

Voice recorders are essential if you choose to experiment with Electronic Voice Phenomena (EVP). Many investigators have claimed that disembodied voices have been caught on a variety of recording devices and the voice recorder has now become an essential piece of any ghost hunter's kit. Recording EVP can range from being very simple to quite complex. I will explain the simple methodology for conducting your own EVP experiment, but please note that this description is in no way comprehensive.

Once you are in your chosen location and have a specific place in which you wish to do your recording you should sit down quietly and start your voice recorder. At the start you should always state your name, the location, the time, persons present (get everyone to say their own name so you have a record of what their voice sounds like on the recording) and also the weather conditions.

An example of some of the authors' paranormal investigation equipment, all contained in a sturdy metal case – essential in order to keep your equipment safe.

Stating the weather is very important as a ghostly moan on your recording may well be the sound of the wind outside if it is particularly windy. All you need to do next is to start asking questions. The quantity of questions is completely up to the individual ghost hunter but remember the quality of your questions is important. You should aim at asking specific questions so that any responses gauged can be checked. As a suggestion I would include asking some of the questions below:

Can you tell me your name please?
Did you live here?
What year is it?
When did you live here?
Can you make three knocks, taps, raps or bangs for me please?

All of these questions could provide you with some interesting information and experiences. Remember after you ask each question to leave a pause before asking your next question, so that any possible ghost that maybe with you can illicit an answer to you. Leaving approximately a ten second pause should suffice. EVP is one of the most interesting and intriguing elements of paranormal investigation and is currently unexplained. Even though some very plausible and possible theories have been offered the jury is still out and the debate between experimenters and critics of EVP continues!

When using your digital camera it is always worth taking random photographs and also asking for any ghosts that maybe haunting the location to stand in front of the camera for you. I have tried this for over ten years, and although I have not had any luck capturing that elusive ghost, your attempts might prove more successful. There are many anomalous photographs in the public domain these days and its worth doing some in-depth research into causes and explanations for some of the most commonly captured phenomena, which usually have a rational explanation. At this point I would like to suggest that you do not count 'orbs' as being paranormal in origin, as there are too many rational explanations for them, ranging from insects to dust, moisture and pollen particles.

If you're going to use a camcorder on your ghost hunt then try to set it at the widest angle so you cover as much of the area in question as possible. It is always best to have more than one camera filming an area. If you manage to capture an apparition on film, then having the image on two cameras is obviously better than just one. In recent years night vision camcorders have become very popular in the ghost hunting community, but unless you're willing to spend in excess of £700 you may find your night vision rather disappointing and will probably need an additional laminator in order for your camera to film well in low-level light conditions. Many companies have actually discontinued their night vision camcorders but if you do have your heart set on getting one then it may be best to search online auction sites or purchase one second-hand, although obviously both of these options come with some risks. Always use brand new tapes and never record over your old tapes even after you have transferred the film to your computer or other media.

A torch is always required as most people conduct their investigations at night time. This is only done to limit the disturbance caused by passers-by and there is no reason at all why you can't ghost hunt in the daytime. In fact, some of my best results have been captured in the broad daylight hours.

I hope that this brief guide, and it is in no means comprehensive, has given you some food for thought in conducting your own ghost hunt. Before you get start searching for the paranormal I would like to offer some simple words of wisdom to bear in mind when ghost hunting:

Have fun and don't lose sight of why you are there.
Always get permission to investigate a location. Trespassing is illegal and gives ghost hunters a bad name so please don't do it!

Always leave the venue in the condition you found it and take all your rubbish away with you.

Stay calm. Many people can become quite over-excited on a ghost hunt and lose their rational thought.

Always remain objective and never jump to conclusions.

Always take a mobile phone with you in case of emergencies and tell someone where you are going and when you expect to be back.

If you would like more information on ghost hunting or would like to attend a ghost hunt then please feel free to visit the website of the Hampshire Ghost Club at www.hampshireghostclub.net and we would be happy to put you in touch with a group in your area. Happy hunting!

Ambresbury Banks, Epping Forest

Built in around 700 BC and spanning some 11 acres stands Ambresbury Banks, an Iron Age hill fort that once afforded shelter and protection to our ancestors. Nowadays the fort is nothing more than a few raised mounds nestled among the sprawling trees that make up Epping Forest.

Although now only a shadow of its former self, Ambresbury Banks is said to be the place where the great leader Boudicca was defeated. It must said at this point though that the exact site of the defeat has never been confirmed and other possible locations exist in the West Midlands, Leicestershire and Warwickshire. The way in which Boudicca passed from this mortal realm is also much debated, as there are conflicting stories. Two Roman historians wrote about Boudicca; Tacitus stated Boudicca poisoned herself whereas Cassius Dio wrote that she fell sick and died. The answers to these questions I fear we will never know.

Regardless of how or exactly where Boudicca's death happened, it is claimed that it is her ghost that has been witnessed wandering through the remains of Ambresbury Banks.

Angel Public House, Braintree

The Angel public house in Bradford Street, Braintree, believes it can trace its roots back to the sixteenth century but 'its history is hard to find', as pub employee Bob told me. He continued, 'we know it was definitely a coaching house in the 1700s', but alas the site's history is proving somewhat troublesome to discover for certain, despite the efforts of the staff and owners.

A medium visited the pub one night and told the staff members that the place was haunted by the ghost of an elderly gentleman. Unfortunately it appears this apparition is only visible to those with a psychic sense for he has yet to be seen by anyone else. The ghost of a woman is alleged to haunt the upstairs of the property and makes her presence known by opening and closing the doors. However the ghost that has been reported here most frequently is not that of a person, but of an animal. Staff members and patrons have, from time to time, glimpsed the ethereal form of a spectral cat. Bob told me that he had worked in pubs all over the area and that they all have a certain amount of vermin ... but not the Angel. Perhaps the pub's ghostly cat keeps the rodents in check?

Beam Valley Country Park, Dagenham

In a peaceful country park in Dagenham, an unassuming piece of land hides a history full of suffering and horrible deaths. You wouldn't know it these days, as there is no trace of the building that once stood here.

Perhaps you will be lucky enough to hear, see or feel something that may hint at what once happened at this now serene, open location. The Beam Valley Country Park was formerly the site of the old Dagenham Hospital and it is said by locals to have a very spooky atmosphere. Some feel they have entered an oppressive area or report feeling uneasy and some even see ghostly figures of the past patients, so if you ever venture to Dagenham's Beam Valley Country Park you may encounter more than you bargain for!

Beeleigh Abbey, Maldon

Founded in the twelfth century for the Premonstratensian order, or white canons, Beeleigh Abbey stood the test of time for over 300 years before it was thrown into turmoil by the dissolution of the monasteries. Beeleigh Abbey was closed and most of its buildings pulled down. After Henry VIII had extracted what he could from the abbey, the lands were granted to Sir John Gate, a man of royal favour who held various influential positions under both Henry VIII and Edward VI, including the post of Sheriff of Essex.

Sir John Gate made an incredible mistake that not only led to his fall from royal grace but also led him to the chopping block on Tower Hill on the 22 August 1553. John's mistake was his support for his friend John Dudley, 1st Duke of Northumberland (1504–1553) in the succession of Lady Jane Gray (1536–1554), the queen who sat on the throne for a mere nine days before she was executed at the Tower of London.

Being an abbey, one would think that the wraiths of the long-gone monks might haunt Beeleigh to this day, but one would be mistaken. It is the soul of the executed Sir John Gate who returns to his former property and it is said that you can witness his spectre and hear his wailing there on 11 and 22 August every year.

Benfleet Conservative Club, Benfleet

The Benfleet Conservative Club is a place somewhat shrouded in mystery, not only in terms of its haunting but also its history. Despite rigorous searches for information on the history of the building that the Conservative Club now inhabits, and has done since 1969, precise details of its construction have remained undiscovered.

At one time the club is believed to have been a manor house in which Lady Hamilton and her famous Royal Navy lover, Lord Horatio Nelson, may have spent time. Although the couple's connection with the building is just a theory, not solidly confirmed in the historical record, the ghost that haunts the club is widely believed to be none other than Lady Hamilton herself.

In 1999 it was reported in the county publication *This is Essex* that former residents Brian and Sandy Wood believed they had encountered the ghost on a number of occasions. Brian witnessed his dog acting rather bizarrely at the door to the spare room, in a manner that suggested that someone had broken into the club. Could the dog have been sensing an unseen presence within the room?

It's not just the dog that was privy to the occasional paranormal occurrence though. One guest who stayed overnight asked the following day if the club was haunted, for he could not shake the feeling that he was constantly being watched by unseen eyes. Sandy Wood herself may have actually seen the spectral form that still haunts here. One day she observed what she can only describe as some sort of shadow. Was it the ghost of Lady Hamilton that Sandy had seen, or could the encounter have a more rational explanation?

Borley Rectory, Braintree

Whenever anyone starts to learn about ghosts and ghost hunting they will always come across the case of Borley Rectory. This highly publicised story has captured many imaginations over the years. We cannot, of course, give a detailed account in this article, nor will we try to prove what is real or not. Borley has many myths attached to it and much of the history is disputed. Here we will just lay out the basic story that has been told over the years. There are many other books dealing with Borley specifically; we can heartily recommend *The Borley Rectory Companion* by Peter Underwood, Eddie Brazil and Paul Adams for one.

On the Essex–Suffolk border lies the small hamlet of Borley. But this quiet little settlement holds a story that is known worldwide. In 1862 Revd H. D. E. Bull, rector of Borley, built the rectory on the site of an old monastery (although this is disputed). By 1927 the last of the Bull family had died (the Revd 'Harry' Foyster Bull 1862–1927). It was during the Bulls' occupancy that the recorded sightings of ghosts started.

Since at least 1900, multiple witnesses claimed to have seen a variety of apparitions. The first recorded sighting was on 28 July 1900 when four of the daughters of the rector reported seeing what they thought was the ghost of a nun not far from the house. The sisters tried to communicate with the figure but it disappeared as they got near to it. The apparent ghost of a nun was also witnessed at later date by neighbours and other family members. The ghostly nun was already known of by the locals. The story goes that she was from a nearby nunnery at Bures (though no nunnery has ever been discovered in Bures, nor in Borley for that matter!) It is said that she tried to elope with a monk from the monastery but she was caught and bricked up in the cellar as a punishment, after which her soul haunted Borley. Along with the poor nun, the monk and the coachmen who were to whisk the couple away were also executed.

The ghost of the nun was said to appear so frequently that Reverend Henry Bull even erected a summer house next to 'nun's walk' so he could watch the ghostly

Borley Rectory photographed in 1892.

apparition. But then, the story goes, the ghost started to scare people with her increasing visitations. Servants didn't stay long in the house due to her activities and the nun would also peer through the rectory windows and frighten guests.

After the last of the Bull family had passed away the building remained empty for a year before the new Reverend, Eric Guy Smith, accompanied by his wife Mabel, took his place at the rectory in late 1928. It was their experiences, perhaps heightened by local rumours, which started the stories of ghosts that we all know today. Shortly after moving into their new home they began to experience strange things, just as the locals had warned. The activity witnessed by the Smiths included phantom footsteps, servant bells ringing of their own accord and whispers and voices from empty rooms. But it was when Mabel found a skull wrapped in a brown paper bag that they finally decided to contact the *Daily Mirror* for help in finding an answer. The *Daily Mirror* contacted renowned ghost hunter and psychical investigator Harry Price to investigate the rectory.

During the writing of this book I was reliably informed of a common misconception; that it was Price who named Borley Rectory 'the most haunted house in England'. In fact, I am told by famed ghost hunter Peter Underwood FRS, that Price actually stopped in nearby Sudbury for directions to the rectory, and the local he asked remarked, 'Oh, you mean the most haunted house in England'. Although Price went on to use the statement in his books on Borley, he certainly was not the source of the claim!

Not long after Price began his investigation he witnessed first-hand some odd goings-on, including a near miss from a flying candlestick. The ghostly activities increased while Price was investigating, including some poltergeist activity such as stones being thrown and objects smashed – understandably, it wasn't long before the Smiths moved out!

The next occupant was Reverend Lionel Foyster and his family. It is with the arrival of this family that the story gets very interesting! Whatever was haunting the building seemed to focus its attentions on Marianne, the wife of Revd Foyster. Amazingly the ghost seemed to be trying to communicate with her, to such an extent that it scrawled messages on the walls. The story goes that this was even witnessed as it happened. Attempts at communication mostly remained unintelligible, though one clearly read, 'Marianne, please help get' and a second read 'light mass prayers'. It was Revd Foyster who attempted the first exorcism at Borley to try to rid the building of its noisy guest! At first it seemed to have worked, but after a while unexplained happenings started up again, such as music being heard from the church opposite, and things got so bad that Foyster and his family moved out. Foyster was the last reverend to serve at Borley.

His departure gave Harry Price the opportunity to move in and really investigate this fascinating location. During these investigations many odd things occurred, including disturbances in rooms that had been sealed, and more stones and pebbles being thrown.

In hindsight, perhaps the most amazing incident was the result of a séance held on 27 March 1938. A ghostly communicator from beyond the grave claimed that the rectory would catch fire in the hallway that night and burn down and a nun's body would be discovered among the ruins. An extraordinary assertion, particularly as nothing happened. Harry Price left the rectory when his one year lease was up. The next occupant, a Captain Gregson, also recorded ghostly goings-on and amazingly,

Borley Church.

exactly eleven months after the séance, the warning came true. It is said that an oil lamp fell and ignited the house. As a final spooky ending, witnesses are said to have seen a ghostly figure wandering through the flames and a man peering through an upstairs window as the fire raged. The blaze consumed the entire house, leaving a burnt-out shell that was eventually levelled. After the fire, the jawbone of a young woman was found in the cellar, seemingly giving credence to the story of the bricked-up nun. In an attempt to end the hauntings the remains were given a Christian burial, but this only seemed to move the activity to the church.

With most attention at the Essex hamlet of Borley being directed to the now demolished rectory, which once sat opposite the church, due to the large amount of national coverage it received, some people haven't heard about the strange events at the church itself. The church, which originally dates to the late twelfth century, and its ornate trees seem peaceful enough, but since the fire that destroyed Borley Rectory, reports of odd goings on at the church have emerged. The Revd Alfred Clifford Henning was one well-known witness. It seems that ghosts that once haunted the rectory may have now moved to the church. Even the nun that once haunted along the famous nun's walk is said to have been sighted within the church grounds. Others have reported strange sounds from within the locked church itself including the organs being heard when by all accounts the building was empty, and footsteps have been heard when no-one was there. Since these early reports many people have investigated the area and have reported odd feelings, strange smells, sightings of figures in the church grounds and some claim to have heard strange noises from within the church itself.

Whether the spirits that once haunted the rooms of the now gone rectory have indeed moved to the church we will maybe never know. Like the story of Borley rectory itself, it may remain an unsolved mystery

Even today, the story is so famous that many people visit this tiny village. The site of the rectory is now occupied by private homes and to my knowledge no activity has been reported there, but people continue to witness strange happenings at the church, such as organ music coming from within when it is locked-up. Are they just caught up in the story or is something supernatural still going on?

The story of Borley has truly captured the minds of many people over the years and even though it is now known that some of what was recorded was at the very least exaggerated, the fact still remains that ghosts were reported at Borley long before the Bull family, Harry Price, or Marianne ever set foot there. We may never know the true extent of what really happened at this now infamous site.

Canvey Island

Although I herald from the county of Hampshire, Canvey Island has a special place in my heart as this is where one branch of my ancestors originated from. Even more incredible is that the 400-year-old house that my great, great, great-grandparents George and Mathanna Mulley occupied is still standing and is in fact known today as the Dutch Cottage on Haven Road.

Canvey Island and its surrounding area has always seemed a place steeped in mystery, so it is fitting that Canvey Island's most famous ghost is somewhat of a mystery also. The ghost of what is suspected to be a Dutchman has been seen in various parts of the island, usually in quieter areas rather than the built-up regions. He is quite conspicuous by the fact that he appears to be carrying a bundle of unknown goods upon his shoulder.

It is also claimed that Knightswick Farm harbours the ghost of a nun who vanishes, not into thin air as is usually expected, but into the ground!

Champions Hall, South Woodham Ferrers

The old manor house located in South Woodham Ferrers has a colourful past. It is known for being the first licensed discothèque in the UK. It was also once at the heart of what is known today as South Woodham Ferrers. When the area was mostly farmland, this house was the family's home and it is the only remaining part of the once thriving farm, as the area surrounding Champions Hall is now a modern housing estate.

Today it is inhabited by a rock band, but they aren't the only occupants of this historic house. Previous tenants and owners have experienced strange feelings and sights. The most common apparition is that of a small girl, who has been felt pushing past people as they go up the stairs. The areas that she is seen in can also, on occasion, completely change in atmosphere. I have experienced this here and I was taken aback by the sudden alteration in how the area felt. At the same time I saw a shadow move past an open door, and shortly afterwards the atmosphere returned to normal. When I asked if this had been observed before, others confirmed that they have had similar experiences of a change in atmosphere for no apparent reason, in different parts of the building. Previous occupants have said they are aware of the ghost girl but are not sure who the young spirit is.

Recently, paranormal investigator and co-founder of Essex Paranormal, Laura Mcphilimey, who lives at Champions Hall, witnessed a full apparition in the master bedroom. She stated that the figure was in the middle of the room and then just vanished. This spectral inhabitant is thought to be the ghost of the grandmother of one of the occupants, whose family have owned the house for many years. It is known that the grandmother died in that room in her old age.

Visiting this house is something of an event; you never know what to expect – some live music courtesy of the band or a visitation from one of the now long-deceased past owners!

Champions Hall, where the ghosts of the past still haunt the modern-day rock band occupants!

Coachman Inn, Earls Colne

When you listen to many of the ghost stories that are told in this day and age they tend to focus on ghostly Victorian ladies, phantom highwaymen, spooky Cavaliers, the spectres of animals who have met grizzly ends and other long-dead spirits. Only very rarely are we privy to a relatively recent haunting. The Coachman Inn at Colchester is one venue that provides such a haunting; their ghost originates from the twentieth century.

Some years ago a former landlord's family came to stay at the hotel and were somewhat perplexed when their young son told them about the man who would appear in his bedroom and often talk with him and even on occasions play with him. At first they assumed it was just the child's imagination. However these thoughts were summarily dismissed when the boy's grandmother also experienced the wraith in the same bedroom.

The most striking thing about the ghost was the description of spectre. He was reported, in the book *Memories of an Essex Ghost Hunter* by Wesley Downes, as wearing 'a singlet, jeans and trainers'. No long, flowing Victorian gowns, phantom coach-and-horses or spectral characters passing through apparently solid walls in this haunting!

Who the ghost is remained a mystery for some time, until a man who was drinking in the Coachman Inn one night was able to solve it. He shocked everyone present by announcing that he had known the gentleman when he was alive, for the ghost was that of his brother. The gentleman who now haunts the place is the son of a former landlord at the Coachman. He was killed in a tragic accident just outside the inn. Following his death, the ghost of the man apparently appears in the room that he once occupied as his bedroom.

Many people think of ghosts as being scary and to be avoided at all costs. Hearing the story of a ghost who now haunts his former bedroom following a tragic and heartbreaking accident, a ghost who talked and played with a child and was generally viewed with a 'smile over his handsome young face', you have to think again and ask yourself, do ghosts really need to be met with so much fear and trepidation? I think not!

Coalhouse Fort, East Tilbury

If you're thinking about visiting a haunted building in Essex you could consider the Coalhouse Fort. In our travels this location has proven to have the most potential to experience something paranormal in Essex, especially for one that is open to the public.

The Coalhouse Fort sits on the edge of the Thames in East Tilbury. There have been defensive structures on this site since 1402, when the first earthworks were laid as defences against a possible French invasion. Since then the fort has been re-built many times, the last of which was finished in 1870s, designed to repel a French invasion that never materialised. Many such forts were built around the UK during this period; they are known today as Palmerston's Follies, after the Lord of the Treasury who commissioned them. The invasion anticipated by Lord Palmerston never came. However, the building did serve its country through both the First and Second World Wars. In particular, the nearby Bowaters Farm anti-aircraft gun emplacement was served by searchlights positioned in and around the fort. One of the main features of the fort at this time were what are known as the 'tunnels', although these are in fact above-ground magazines that held the ammunition for the huge guns that were situated on the floors above. The site was eventually sold to Thurrock Urban District Council in 1962. The area was then left derelict, and it was during this period of abandonement, it is said by some locals and staff, that the tunnels were used for so-called 'black magic' rituals. Some evidence seems to back this up; for example, satanic graffiti appears on the walls of some of the tunnel rooms. It has been suggested that these rituals may be the cause of the fort's supernatural occurrences.

The Coalhouse Project obtained a lease on the building in 1983 and has been slowly and lovingly breathing new life into the site ever since. It has become a great venue for re-enactors and military lovers alike. The fort has kept the military theme and houses several military vehicles and an Aviation Museum that exhibits, among other items, parts from crashed Second World War planes. A lot of these items originate from the historic Battle of Britain and were found in the local area. It is also from this period of the fort's history that the ghosts seem to originate. Could it be that the care and restoration work that has gone into the site has caused ghosts of the past to show their presence again?

Since the site has been undergoing restoration, members of staff have experienced some strange goings-on. Many report feeling, or even seeing, a definite presence next to them, only to find that no-one is there. Over the last six years a number of ghost investigation groups have spent nights at the fort and have experienced paranormal encounters. The first group to investigate the location was the Ghost Club, the oldest investigating group in the UK. Since then many teams have ventured to the old Victorian fort in search of the unknown. They bring with them a range of equipment in the hopes of collecting evidence of the paranormal activity that has been reported by so many people at this historic site. Many of the investigators who have spent nights here claim to have experienced much of the same activity that has been reported by the fort's volunteer staff.

Although some of the fort is out of bounds due to the poor state of the building, such as the 'quad', which used to be living quarters, there are still many areas that are open to investigators. Some seem to be more active than others. One area that interests me personally, due to the number of times something odd was encountered there, is Room 24 in the tunnels. Here I share two accounts from my own experiences in this room while investigating the forts with Essex Paranormal.

In the first instance, I and a small investigation team were walking from the latrines towards the centre of the tunnels. As I was turning the corner I could see a ghostly figure of what I believed to be a 1940s soldier standing in Room 24. The figure looked round at me, bending slightly with his lower half hidden in the doorway. I could clearly see the outline in the torchlight. It was so clear that I was able to identify the uniform as one typically worn in the 1940s by privates and NCOs. He also had a beret in the style worn by soldiers from that era. Without thinking, I moved quickly towards the room but found no-one and heard nothing; the room was empty. We searched the rest of the tunnels and found no-one who shouldn't have been there and all of my group were accounted for. That experience certainly made my night, and it wouldn't be the last time I experienced some odd goings-on in Room 24!

The second story regarding Room 24 again took place during an investigation with Essex Paranormal. This time we had a medium with us who was helping us out with our research. All was going as it normally does on such nights; people were taking photographs, taking notes of such things as temperature and electromagnetic field readings. The first half an hour was mainly uneventful, but then the medium seemed to pick up on something or someone. The team observed

Coalhouse Fort.

and made notes of what the medium relayed to us. He thought the energy he was feeling was male and of military background. This was unsurprising, of course, as we were in a known ex-military establishment. But what did surprise me and the team was that when the medium seemed to be getting strong energy from what he said was a spirit, a powerful gust of wind suddenly came from the tunnels into Room 24. I was sitting in the entrance between the dark tunnels and the room. The wind was cold with some force behind it and certainly gave me a shock. We recorded a tangible drop in temperature of 1.5°c on our thermometers. The wind, once it had entered the room, seemed to circle the group before dissipating! A member of staff seemed shocked too. Having been down the tunnels countless times, she stated that the strength of the wind wasn't natural. We were not near any of the entrances and the weather that night was calm and cold with a very slight breeze; certainly there was not enough wind outside to cause what we all felt inside. We could not explain where such a gust came from. Some people in the group noted that it rushed into the room as the medium said the energy he was sensing from the spirit was gaining in strength. It left even the more rational of us thinking!

Another memorable night for me, due entirely to the clarity of the event, is that which I recount now. The fact is, no matter how logical or how scientific you are, there is really no rational explanation for what we experienced.

It occurred during a vigil with me and three members of coalhouse staff. We had just entered the lighting tunnels not far from the entrance by the large ramp. We all had torches on and could see our immediate surroundings quite clearly. The group were all startled when we all heard footsteps following us. They were so clear that I had initially thought the steps were those of another member of staff who was perhaps running late; I was now to learn that this wasn't the case. The steps came round the corner and walked in our direction. All of our torches were still on and no-one could be seen. All being ghost hunters, we had huge smiles, as it is this type of activity we strive to experience. The clear sound of the steps then stopped in front of us and a heavy sigh was heard by all. The disembodied steps then walked off in the direction they had come from! This was a very exciting moment as no-one who was there could rationally explain it, and the sounds were so distinct, not in the distance or faded but very clear and apparent. We had a digital camera with us, which did produce photographs of a huge number of balls of lights known to many as orbs, but as the location is incredibly dusty and damp they cannot be used as proof of paranormal activity. However, for those present no further proof is needed that what we witnessed was not explainable by known science.

This experience fits with other reports of the ghost of a lady named Elizabeth, or Beth as she is known to the fort's volunteers. The daughter of a captain who was once stationed at the fort, she is said to have been somewhat promiscuous. When she has been seen she is reported to wear a powder-blue dress and to have a coquettish look about her. Many people have also noted a smell of violets and lavender accompanying her when she makes an appearance. It is said she has a thing for blond soldiers and if you do not fit the bill she sighs and walks off in disappointment! In fact the sighs are one of the most common reports in my experience, heard in various parts of the fort by many different people. She has also been heard to giggle when the mood takes her.

A written account of the ghosts of the Coalhouse Fort wouldn't be complete without the next amazing yet terrifying incident. It happened during an investigation run by Ghosts UK, one of the UK's oldest established ghost investigating groups.

All was going well and during a break some members went to their cars to retrieve some items. One lady, a Ghosts UK core team member, was on her way back to the base room when she was heard to scream. Running up the ramp that takes you to the first floor, she entered the base room in quite a state, visibly upset and shaken. Once the poor lady had calmed down she recounted her experience. She said that halfway up the ramp she heard footsteps in the gravel behind her. Looking back to see who it was, she saw a faceless dark figure. Frightened, she ran up the ramp and the figure ran after her and she heard the footsteps behind her accelerate. She couldn't continue the vigil that night and was quite shaken at the experience. The leaders of the group quickly decided to do a search of the entire site, to make sure no-one was there who should not have been. Over an hour later, after an exhaustive search of every room, nothing was found. The main doors were locked and security had seen nothing. It is indeed a mystery as to who or what this figure was, but it certainly left its impression on the poor lady!

One area that we don't usually have access to is the Aviation Museum, but during one investigation we were kindly given permission to spend some time in this gem of a museum, which, although small, holds some fascinating exhibits from the Second World War. While we only spent a couple of hours there, it became apparent that these rooms had great potential. During the first part of the vigil, at which we had several cameras set up and a medium helping us out, a stone was thrown at two investigators with some force. The sound of the stone hitting one of the exhibits and the reactions of both investigators were caught on video camera. Something else strange was picked up on at the same time. There was a profound temperature change and some then felt there was a presence in the room. This was a great start to the evening for us.

The medium helping us then correctly identified two brothers both of whom had served with the RAF and died during the Second World War. The curator of the museum confirmed what the medium had said and also added that this information was very hard to find. After the vigil we left several cameras running along with an audio recording from the 1940s and shut the doors for an hour. On reviewing these tapes we found a few loud bangs followed by a flash of light which seemed to be in response to what was being played on the recording.

The Aviation Museum houses many aircraft parts from the Second World War, mostly from the Battle of Britain. The parts are from aircraft that came down in the local area, in which brave young pilots lost their lives. Some have theorised that the energy of the lost souls are attached or embedded into the crashed parts. Could this be what is going on in the Coalhouse Aviation Museum? The curator we met told us that when he came to work at the fort he was not a believer in ghosts and the paranormal, but he now believes, having experienced the intense feeling of being watched, as if a person was almost looking over his shoulder, only to find he was alone. He had also experienced odd goings-on down the notorious tunnels.

Sue Oliver who worked at the fort has recalled some of the interesting events that occurred during her time at Coalhouse Fort. She recounted to me an amazing event during an investigation in one of the casemates. The small team included Sue, a medium and an investigator who filmed the vigil. Sue and the medium stood quietly face-to-face for five minutes, with the investigator in the corner filming. After this period they noticed some footprints beside them. The casemate floor was dry and dusty and the footprints were damp as if someone had stood in a puddle. On further investigation there were no other damp footprints anywhere to be seen. Added to this, the camera didn't seem to record when the footsteps appeared; only static was seen during playback!

Sue also remembers setting up for the annual Hallowe'en event (a fright night purely for the entertainment for visitors), when heard what she thought was the sound of drums. She checked whether anyone was there but saw nothing and returned to her work. The sounds got louder so again she checked for movement or lights from other people, but again she saw nothing. The noise became louder still and seemed to be coming from one side of the tunnels before passing right by her and continuing down the tunnels. She stated that she very quickly went the other way!

All in all, many investigators and staff have experienced odd things at Coalhouse Fort that are, for the moment, beyond explanation. Hopefully the ongoing investigations will one day find out exactly who or what is haunting this location!

Colchester Castle, Colchester

Colchester's Norman castle sits on the foundations of the Roman temple that was once Britain's capital. This site has seen much bloodshed and pain during its long history, from the attacks of Boudicca in AD 60, which left as many as 30,000 people dead, to Matthew Hopkins' reign of terror, when 400 women were put to death after the Witchfinder General gave evidence at Colchester Castle.

The castle itself is believed to have started life in 1076 (although some historians believe construction began around the 1090s) during the reign of William I, more commonly known as William the Conqueror. The keep of Colchester Castle is the largest in Europe and its design was later used for the infamous prison and royal palace, the Tower of London.

The long and varied history of the castle is perfect for ghost stories, tales of horrific murder and torture being among those that make Colchester Castle so fascinating. The main recorded ghost story is that of Quaker James Parnell. Mr Parnell clashed with the authorities of the time because of his religious beliefs. He was subsequently levied with a fine of £40 which he refused to pay and was therefore imprisoned. He died in the prison of the castle on 10 April 1656; Having been forced to climb a rope every time that he wanted food, he eventually fell to his death. Since then his ghost is said to haunt the dungeon. One legend states that a brave soul dared to stay overnight in the dungeon for a bet and left the castle a nervous wreck!

Today, a few ghost investigation groups have spent nights in this fascinating place to see if there really is any truth to these stories but it does seem possibly to be a much embellished myth. Some groups have reported odd goings-on and feelings of not being alone, but this is no surprise when you look at the turbulent history of the castle!

Right: Colchester Castle seen across the fish pond in Castle Park.

Below: The castle walls.

Colchester Castle.

Cross Keys Hotel, Saffron Walden

The Cross Keys Hotel in Saffron Walden has a very interesting history, as indeed does Saffron Walden itself, having been the headquarters of Oliver Cromwell, the leader of the parliamentarian faction during the English Civil War (1642–1651).

Known in Cromwell's time as the Whalebone, the hotel dates back to the fourteenth century and its haunting is well known. In Jack Hallam's now famous book, *Haunted Inns of England*, it is reported that landlords were privy to the phantom footfalls of the hotel's spectral occupant around Christmas time 1963 and again in 1964. The 'very heavy, slow, ponderous footsteps are heard from a corridor which has a blind end', usually between 11 p.m. and midnight.

Such well-documented incidents are of extreme use in paranormal investigation and research, but as the last known events occurred in the 1960s I began to wonder if anything had been reported in recent years. I was lucky enough to speak to Colin Smith from Ghost Hunt Team Essex who investigated the Cross Keys in March 2007 and again in February 2009.

Colin told me how his investigation of the hotel transpired:

This came about simply from a picture of a 'ghost' photographed in a room at the old Cross Keys Hotel in Saffron Walden, Essex. After discussing room rates with the owner, permission was granted for the team to hold an investigation in two rooms at the hotel. The team jumped at the chance!

The Cross Keys stands in the centre of the town at the junction of the High Street and King Street. It is a wonderful half-timbered building which dates at least from the fourteenth century with later additions. Its haunted reputation has been mentioned in several local books plus an American ghost hunting guide and a programme on Anglia TV. The main ghost is supposed to be a Civil War soldier and the most haunted room is Number 6. This was to be an all-night vigil. We started at 11.30 p.m. and ended at around 4.45 a.m.

Cross Keys Hotel in Saffron Walden. Photograph © Colin Smith.

Throughout the investigation there appear to have been some occurrences that defy rational explanation, according to the reports written by Ghost Hunt Team Essex. The smell of garlic, inexplicable flashing lights, changes in temperature, sensations of being touched and even the psychic impression by three individuals of a black shadow that appeared to the group during their vigil in Room 6. During the early part of the team's investigation at the hotel, some of the mediums felt that they could feel the presence of the Witchfinder General, Matthew Hopkins, and the black shadow in Room 6 witnessed by the team was attributed to this most dastardly of souls. Unfortunately, to date, there is no historical evidence to suggest that Matthew Hopkins ever visited the Cross Keys Hotel or had any connection to the venue.

On the upside though, it does appear that Ghost Hunt Team Essex may have solved the mystery of the ghostly photograph that drew them to the hotel in the first place. 'Sadly, it appeared that whoever took the picture must have faked it, because although the room is active, it became very apparent how the photograph was achieved once we were in the room. On the floor in the same location was a kettle on an extension cord. It seemed more logical to us that the photographer had snapped the steam of the kettle boiling as it resembled a human shape,' concluded Colin.

Garrison Arms, Shoeburyness

This short story comes from my own childhood. When I was a young teen my mother worked at a local pub. We knew it then as Captain Mannering's, after the fictional character in the highly popular sitcom *Dad's Army*. The misspelling was a mistake by the sign writer, as any fan of *Dad's Army* will know that the character's name was spelt Mainwaring!

The Garrison Arms (formerly Captain Mannering's) in Shoeburyness.

The Clock Tower at Shoeburyness Barracks.

Today the pub is known as the Garrison Arms. The building itself has its roots in the military as part of the gunnery school sited in Shoeburyness. It was built in 1898 as a military hospital and paid for by public subscription in memory of seven soldiers who were killed in an accidental explosion at the barracks in 1885.

As I stated, my mother used to work there in the early 1990s and she told me that the cellar would sometimes smell of the odour you get when visiting a hospital, antiseptic and the like, and the place would have a strange atmosphere to it. Now my mother wasn't one for believing in ghosts, but she couldn't explain the smell and atmosphere. Could some of the chemicals be embedded into the brickwork and be slowly releasing themselves over time? Could the past of this building be refusing to go? Could the trauma and illness that was experienced by so many now be part of the building? Hopefully these supernatural events will continue at the Garrison Arms and maybe some new ones will even occur that might give us some more clues as to what is being experienced here.

Grays Beach, Thurrock

The website of Thurrock Council states that Grays Beach is 'a fantastic place to visit at any time'. However there are some who certainly would not recommend a walk along this haunted beach!

Deaths connected to the ocean are common, therefore it comes as no surprise to find that some have lost their lives in the area of Grays Beach and the ghosts witnessed here could very well be connected to those whose lives were lost in tragic circumstances.

The now sadly defunct Thurrock Paranormal group reports on its website that the main story concerning Grays Beach is the apparition of a sailor who has been seen taking the wheel of a phantom boat in the area. There are also other stories describing a phantom woman, with long grey hair and wearing a white shawl, who has been likened to a banshee; she once took to the air before rushing towards a man walking his dog, screaming as she went!

A further story concerned a young man who was struck on the head while walking and when he turned to discover what it was that had hit him, or indeed who had thrown it, he was startled to see a rubbish bin hurtling towards him. He promptly ducked out of the way and when he looked again to see where the bin had gone he found it back in its original place, still firmly fixed to the ground!

The idyllic but haunted beach at Grays.

Great Chalvedon Hall, Pitsea

I first became aware of the haunted history of Great Chalvedon Hall in Pitsea when a friend and fellow ghost hunter was told of its notoriety as a haunted venue by a local woman who had held many a clairvoyant night on the premises.

Sheila Norton-Badrul told me that the pub had experienced various levels of paranormal activity for some years. I asked Sheila if she could me more about the hall, its history and its ghostly residents.

As far as the building goes, it is known as Great Chalvedon Hall and it is a Grade II listed building. Prior to it being converted to a pub in the 1960s, it belonged to a husband and wife team of solicitors and during the war years it was used as a children's home. The hall at this time housed children from London who had been bombed out during the blitz and had lost relatives in the horrific conflict, hence why some of the poltergeist activity and manifestations witnessed here have been children. I have previously interviewed the bar staff who had witnessed a manifestation of a school boy in a cap and 1940s-style clothing and I also met with one of the men who lived in the children's home as a boy.

When the house was owned by the solicitors they had a German Shepherd dog and it flatly refused to go into the main living area; in fact it wouldn't even go past the kitchen.

Perhaps the dog was aware of the ethereal residents who remained hidden from the view of the living occupants, a situation commonly suggested and felt in the genre of hauntings and ghosts. It often seems that animals are privy to much more than we mere humans!

So what of the history of Great Chalvedon Hall before the Second World War? Are there any clues in the early years of the location's history that could possibly be the originating cause of the ghosts here? Sheila said:

There are links back to the time of Henry II and rumours abound that it was used by Henry VIII for a hunting lodge, though research by a historian friend of mine suggested that many manor houses boasted this to gain more kudos. During the time of English Civil War (1642–1651) there was a priest hole located in the building that was connected by a tunnel to St Michael's Church in Pitsea. I understand there have been, over the years, reports of a phantom coach and horses being seen at the front of the building, but no names of witnesses or dates relating to these phenomena seem to have survived

Many families have lived and worked in the house; farmers and their families and staff. Several persons have met their end here, something confirmed by several mediums. They have said the hall is very active. One mentioned a monk, but I can't confirm that.

One of the most frequently witnessed ghosts is that of a scullery maid who worked at the hall and used to live in the attic bedroom. She has been described as wearing a white mop cap and apron with a dark, long-sleeved dress.

So with all this paranormal phenomena occurring has Sheila witnessed a ghost herself?

'I have not witnessed any apparitions here personally, but I have connected with a number of spirit entities that seem to occupy various areas of the building. I have a name of Alice Pleshey, who I believe to be the scullery maid, and also a Master James Gaunt,' she says.

Although Sheila had not witnessed any ghosts with her own eyes at Great Chalvedon Hall, I felt that surely this psychic information at least gave us something to check in the historical record. But, alas, the information could not be confirmed as the census information doesn't go back far enough, and most of the old records were destroyed by fire many years ago. So even if the ghosts of Great Chalvedon Hall appeared to us this evening and told us their names, dates and events in their lives, this could not be checked in the historical record and so none of it could be confirmed for certain. The hall, I am sure, will remain an enigmatic mystery for many years to come.

Hadleigh Castle, Hadleigh

Overlooking Canvey Island stand the remains of Hadleigh Castle. Construction of the castle began in 1230 during the reign of Henry III for nobleman Hubert De Burgh, 1st Earl of Kent (1160–1243). The castle was in an unfortunate state of decline and general abandonment from 1551 onwards when it was sold to Lord Rich of Leez Priory who plundered the castle for its stone.

Nowadays, the castle is just another romantic ruin on the landscape of England, but it appears that although the castle of long ago is all but vanished one of its past residents remains. The apparition of a lady dressed in white has been witnessed but her identity and her reasons for remaining behind in the mortal realm remain a mystery. It is said that the ghost, known locally as the White Lady, spoke one morning to a milkmaid called Sally from the nearby castle farm. The ghost told Sally to meet her again at the castle at midnight but the girl was understandably too frightened to go. The next morning the White Lady confronted Sally once again and, annoyed that she had been disobeyed, she hit the milkmaid around the head, almost dislocating her neck. After this the girl became known as 'wry-neck Sal'.

The apparition of John 'Cunning' Murrell is also claimed to have been witnessed collecting herbs that grow around the castle. His story is featured in a later chapter.

The remains of Hadleigh Castle.

Hangman's Hill, High Beech

For many years now Hangman's Hill has been a place of mystery and intrigue, not only for the locals but for people from all over the world.

Legend surrounds the hill. It is claimed that centuries ago there stood upon the hill a hangman's noose where executions took place. Being a place of such trauma and terror it is not surprising to discover that people visiting the area over many years have had strange and sometimes unnerving encounters in the area. People come from far and wide to test out Hangman's Hill.

It is said that if you park your car on Hangman's hill, put the gear in neutral and place your handbrake on, your car mysteriously, and quite shockingly, rolls not down the hill but up it! Local myth states this is due to the ghost of the hangman dragging the cars up Hangman's Hill, although why he would choose to do such a thing is baffling! In fact, a little research easily puts this wondrous mystery to rest. Hangman's Hill appears to be an uphill slope. However, a simple experiment with a spirit level will show any investigator that the hill actually in fact slopes downwards. The appearance of the uphill slope is simply an optical illusion, and a very convincing one indeed!

Although there is no phantom hangman dragging the cars and their hapless passengers up the hill, there are still other unusual experiences to be had in the area. One of these is the appearance of a man who has been witnessed on at least two occasions flagging down cars. As the cars slow down for the man he runs off into the woods. Is he trying to show the passing motorists something of interest? Is he a phantom in need of help? Or could the encounter have a mundane and less ethereal explanation?

Harwich Redoubt, Harwich

The Harwich Redoubt was built as part of a defence system in 1808. At that time the enemy that threatened England was the Napoleonic forces. Included in these defences are twenty-nine Martello towers that were strung across the East Anglian coast. The fort is circular in shape and in its day would have had completely uninterrupted views from the hill it sits on. It is even said that French prisoners of war were used as labour in its construction.

The fort never saw any action or fired a shot in anger. In the 1920s the fields below, which had previously been kept clear of any obstructions, were built up as the land was purchased by the local council. The most interesting period in the history of Harwich Redoubt, at least in the authors' view, is the Second World War, when it was brought back into service briefly as a detention centre for British prisoners facing trial. It was in this period that some of the prisoners left markings and graffiti that can be seen to this day.

The Harwich Redoubt is now a museum and listed as an ancient monument; the restoration and maintenance of this historic place is ongoing. Many of those who visit today have said that past soldiers have failed to leave! Some of the phenomena witnessed by visitors, staff and investigators include footsteps from areas of the fort that are empty and strange hot and cold spots in some of the rooms; there are even reports of people feeling the touch of unseen hands.

One of the main ghosts of the redoubt is that of a headless soldier that it is said walks the grounds. The poor soldier is said to have lost his head not in combat but during the mounting of one of the huge guns, which slipped its ropes, instantly decapitating the man. Maybe this very quick death could explain why he is still here. Perhaps his soul has not come to terms with the fact that his death came so swiftly and unexpectedly. In my own experience military sites have demonstrated more potential for activity than other types of location and this site seems to be no different!

Harwich Redoubt Fort.

Kelvedon Hatch Nuclear Bunker, Braintree

Hidden in the Essex countryside is an important part of our recent history. Built deep inside a hill is a once secret nuclear bunker designed to act as one of the hubs of activity to keep the country running if the horror of nuclear war was ever to hit England.

The Kelvedon Hatch nuclear bunker was built in 1952 as an RAF ROTOR station and upgraded in the early sixties to RGHQ (regional headquarters). In case of nuclear attack the continuation of government would have taken place here. The site itself would have housed up to 600 personnel, both military and civilians. Above ground the only signs of the bunker are a large antenna that sits on top of the hill and a small bungalow housing the guard room and entrance, which starts just behind the 1.5-ton blast door down a dark, concrete corridor.

The site was decommissioned in the early 1990s and the land returned to the original landowners. It is now a very popular museum where many people, staff and visitors alike, have reported strange goings-on.

My own experience at this location was very interesting. We arrived to the beautiful sight of thousands of bluebells in bloom in the woods surrounding the site. The bungalow which houses the bunker entrance belies the huge complex within. Upon entering the bunker the atmosphere changed, although it had nothing to do with any ghosts, more to do with leaving the visually stunning woods for a dark, grey, concrete military bunker. Our team did the usual tour to get our bearings and to take baseline tests and general photographs, What became apparent was how big the place was; you certainly had no idea such a place was tucked away in these sleepy surroundings. During the initial walk around, a few people in our team said they thought they saw shadows moving in the corners in what is called the BBC room and had felt the air of people busily working around them, and this would not be the last time such things were felt here.

The entrance to Kelvedon Hatch nuclear bunker cleverly disguised as a bungalow.

After a briefing we set up and started our first vigil and this is when things got weird. We had two teams, one on the upper level and my team on the lower floor in what was once a plotting room. During our vigil we recorded and heard the sounds of footsteps directly above us, on what sounded like wooden floors. The footsteps sounded like a single person, walking slowly. What we discovered during post-investigation research was that in the bunker's original structure as an RAF ROTOR station it had a raised wooden balcony above the main plotting table, but today those wooden floors have gone and reinforced concrete floors have replaced them. When the vigil had finished we met up with the other team to compare notes. It transpired that at the same time as we had heard the footsteps the other group had also recorded hearing footsteps walk past the room they were in, although no-one could be seen through the window as the footsteps passed.

Later that evening we held another vigil in what were said to be dormitories, two rooms with bunks. We carried out the usual checks on temperature and got settled for the vigil. During our time in there we could hear what sounded like distant talking, like a room full of women busily working and chatting. We all stood, stunned and silent, listening to this distant noise. It was a very surreal experience and no matter how hard we tried we could not find out where the sound was coming from, or it would suddenly stop when we tried to search! It could be described as being on the periphery of our senses, just out of our range but noticeable enough to stop and make you listen. I can imagine that during the day when the tours are on this type of activity might be missed by most. As a side note, during this time we noted that our thermometers showed a very fast temperature drop of 4°c in a few minutes from only one of the rooms. Again we could find no reason for such a change.

My own personal opinion is that when station was in full operation there were times when nuclear war seemed imminent and the thoughts and fears, especially of the civilian workers, seem to have been imprinted into the building. Several of us noticed similar sounds and thoughts in the medical bay, as if there was a great deal of activity going on just a few rooms away but everytime we went to find the source of the noise nothing but silence would fill the air.

Many other groups have spent the night with similar experiences at Kelvedon Hatch; footsteps, strange sensations and feelings of people working hard in this place that would have once been such a hive of activity have all been reported. Every now and again, it seems, the building replays some of its past to those

Kelvedon Hatch bunker entrance.

Has the intense emotion that was
felt by staff at Kelvedon Hatch
nuclear bunker somehow imprinted
itself into the very fabric of the
structure?

The government
floors of Kelvedon
Hatch nuclear
bunker. In the
event of a nuclear
war it was from
here that Great
Britain would have
fought on.

willing to listen. It is almost as if we are witnessing the fears of the people who once worked here, scared of the very real possibility of a nuclear war and all the horror that entails. I can understand why this place seems to buzz with energy and at times you certainly don't feel alone!

There is also a story that a workman building the bunker fell into a huge area of wet concrete that had just been laid. It is said his body was never found and there is a theory that some of the activity experienced by people could be down to this individual who, for all we know, is still buried deep inside the walls! The bunker is a fascinating building from an amazing part of our history, and one that I look forward to returning to one day.

Lagenhoe Church, Colchester

Lagenhoe is a small village hiding away in the district of Colchester but it is very well known to those who have a passion for researching haunted places.

In my previous books I have always tried not to include haunted venues that are no longer there. After all, there's no point whetting your appetite with an amazing collection of ghost stories only for you to read that the sites no longer exist. However, with the writing of *Paranormal Essex* I have made an exception on two accounts, for they simply cannot be left out of any book dealing with the ghosts and hauntings of Essex. Those two places are Borley Rectory, of course, and Lagenhoe church (the latter I will assume is not known to many readers of this book).

The reasons I have decided to include the stories connected to Lagenhoe church are twofold. Firstly, the events that occurred at the church, sometimes in the presence of multiple witnesses, cannot be overlooked and secondly I am a friend of one of the gentlemen that conducted extensive investigations at the church in the 1940s and 1950s and am confident in the testimony and tales he recounted to me on numerous occasions during our late-night conversations on the paranormal.

Lagenhoe church was rebuilt in 1886 after sustaining damage during the now famous 'Great English Earthquake' that hit the Colchester area on 22 April 1884. Modern study of the earthquake's history estimates the quake to have been 4.6 on the Richter scale. My friend, the Revd John C. Denning, started his research and investigations into claims of the paranormal at the church in the late 1940s, after the Revd E. A. Merryweather started to report some unusual occurrences. Revd Denning investigated the church alongside fellow investigator and friend Peter Underwood. Later, Denning would have to keep his interest and involvement in the paranormal somewhat quiet; his career as an Anglican priest meant that his involvement in such projects would have caused conflict with his superiors had it been discovered. However, during the initial investigations at Lagenhoe Denning was working for the Foreign Office, so a clash of religious opinions was not an issue.

The best way in which I can convey the whole host of assorted phenomena experienced at Lagenhoe church is to draw extensively on both my conversations with Mr Denning and extracts from his excellent book, *The Restless Spirits of Lagenhoe Church*, which details many of the ghostly events that took place at the church.

One of the earliest things that the Revd E. A. Merryweather commented on was the 'peculiar and by no means pleasant atmosphere' of the church. This was mainly just the vicar's impression of the church after having been there for a couple of months, but it seems these feelings were the precursor to some amazing paranormal events.

Revd Merryweather reported on one occasion, in 1947, that while practising the hymns at the church organ he felt as if he was being watched. In fact he stated that the person who was watching him was standing right behind him and he spun round to speak to the person only to find that the church was completely deserted.

On Sunday 18 July 1948 at exactly 11 a.m. (the time is known precisely as the sung communion service was being held) Revd Merryweather and his entire congregation were witness to what sounded like 'someone throwing clods of earth at the (vestry) door'. The service was not halted at this time but later inspection found no evidence of anything having been thrown at the door. This event occurred again on numerous occasions and always at the same point during the service. No explanation was ever found.

On Thursday 19 August 1948 Mrs Barnes, the housekeeper for Revd Merryweather, was cleaning the church when she commented on the sensation of an evil presence within the church. She claimed that it felt as if 'someone was near who wanted to kill me'. On this occasion Mrs Barnes left the church as she couldn't shake the nasty feeling that she was being subjected to.

On Sunday 28 November 1948. Revd Merryweather entered the church to prepare for a service and at once noted the damp atmosphere in the church and decided to light a fire in the church stove and try to warm the place up a little. He placed his Biretta, a box-type cap, on a pole to air it out a little and was shocked to watch the Biretta start to spin around on the pole on its own. Merryweather was confident the hat had been placed on the pole in a stationary position and that no draught was responsible for causing the hat to move in such a fashion.

You may be thinking by now that feelings of being watched are common and are not necessarily paranormal, and you would be quite correct. You may also be thinking that the sounds of thumping at the vestry door could be attributed to mischievous children creating the noises and escaping in plenty of time as they knew full well that the adults would not disturb their communion. Perhaps the hat spinning was created by the warm thermals from the lit stove. Again, it is a possibility. But what followed the hat spinning incident cannot be explained by any logical means. I reproduce the exact description contained within John Denning's book, as this most accurately describes what occurred next:

> Scarcely had the rector recovered from his astonishment at this intriguing incident [the Biretta spinning] when he was startled to hear, all of a sudden, a woman's voice somewhere in the church utter, quite distinctly, the words: 'you are a cruel man'! In amazement, and thinking at first that someone was addressing him, Mr Merryweather swung round fully expecting to find someone had entered the building. But not a bit of it – the church was as empty as before. The mysterious voice died away, and there followed an eerie stillness. It was then that the rector noticed, lying on the floor behind him, his own large pocketknife, with the big blade opened and pointing towards him! 'How on earth did that get there?' he thought to himself, as he picked up the knife and examined it. A moment or two earlier it had been reposing harmlessly in the depth of his trouser pocket (in which incidentally there was definitely no hole).

To usher out the year 1948 the Reverend was privy to two more occurrences that baffled him. Both events occurred in December. One day while making his way up the nave the priest was somewhat startled to hear a man cough! It was so loud it actually made Merryweather jump. A couple of weeks later, on 19 December, Merryweather entered the church to find a sparrow flapping at the church windows. Somewhat confused as to how the small bird got into the building in the first place he decided to set about the task of setting the bird free. As the Reverend reached up to open the window he was astounded to witness the bird simply vanish right in front of his eyes!

The next and most interesting event in the paranormal history of Lagenhoe church took place on Sunday 21 August 1949, when in the middle of a Holy Communion service Revd Merryweather looked up to witness the apparition of a woman who apparently emerged from the north wall of the church. When pressed by John Denning as to the description of this female ghostly form, Mr Merryweather was very specific. He stated that the woman was aged '20–30, 5 foot 6 inches in height and also seemed to walk with a slight stoop'. Alas the reverend could not describe the woman's features.

For the next decade, paranormal events continued at the church and regular reports were made and investigated of mysterious footsteps, phantom smells, displacement of objects, doors being locked and unlocked on their own, strange thumping sounds at the doors and the smashing of glassware inside the church.

Revd Denning's investigations continued at the church and culminated in a series of séances where the reverend believed that his investigation team contacted the ghosts of a lady named Mary Felicity and a gentleman by the name of Sir Robert. These séances led the team to believe that Sir Robert had murdered Mary Felicity in the church sometime in the seventeenth century and it was this dastardly deed that had caused the church to become haunted for so many years. As a result of these communication sessions between the ghosts and the mediums at Lagenhoe church, the decision was reached to try to bring peace to the restless souls of Mary Felicity and Sir Robert. An exorcism, not a traditionally based one, I should add, but one more akin to the beliefs of the Spiritualist movement, was performed with all participants confident in the fact that these ghosts that had haunted Lagenhoe church for so long were now finally laid to rest.

I would dearly love to investigate the church but alas this is not a possibility as it was closed in 1955 and finally demolished in 1963.

Little Walden, Uttlesford

RAF Little Walden was a Second World War airfield that was active in the years 1944–1958 and was used by both the Royal Air Force and the United States Army Air Force. There has been one ghost reported at this former airfield. The apparition of a headless airman has been seen haunting the area, which no doubt witnessed the man's downfall.

Maltings, Saffron Walden

One of the oldest buildings in the picturesque village of Saffron Walden is the old maltings. The 600-year-old oak beams and uneven floors give the building real character and a feeling of past eras which fit in with the rest of this stunningly beautiful village.

Inside the building there are many original features including part of the medieval great hall and part of the pulley system used to lift the bags of malt to the top rooms; the beamed rooms are just steeped in history and hauntings. Many people who have visited this place say that not only does the place have the feel of past times but that some of the past occupants are still hanging around making themselves known from time to time.

The most foreboding part of the building has to be the dark, eerie cellar. During an investigation at the Maltings in 2004 we heard unexplained loud bangs and movement from parts of the cellar. Similar events have since been recorded by other witnesses. Shadowy movements have also been seen. Very odd electromagnetic fluctuations, which seem to respond to questions, have been experienced and during one investigation a statement was made asking for any spirits present to make a noise and show us their presence in the building. Our meter went off the chart, before going to zero, but not on just the one occasion; this event repeated itself several times to the complete and utter amazement of the entire team!

One night a guest was staying over and shortly after arriving at the house decided to visit the toilet. Making his way to the toilet area the guest, who wishes to remain anonymous, was suddenly overcome with a sensation of dizziness and falling. He said it was if he had fallen into a hole. Feeling a little perplexed at the occurrence, the guest decided to go and seek out the manager and tell him about the event. The manager at the time informed the guest that the spot where the dizziness and falling sensation had occurred was in fact in an area of the building where centuries ago a worker using the pulley system from the upper levels, had fallen from the top of the building into the open cellar! Could it be the ghost of this former employee that people have encountered in the area of the cellar?

Many groups have left the Maltings impressed by the paranormal activity and feeling they get from this haunted building.

The historic Maltings building in Saffron Walden

Matthew Hopkins,
Various Parts of Essex

Throughout history there have always been characters who will be remembered for their acts of cruelty and barbarism. Hanging Judge Jefferies, Henry VIII, Jack the Ripper and Dick Turpin are all names that send a shudder down the spine of most when their heinous acts are discussed. Essex has its own very special sadistic personality though...the self-proclaimed Witchfinder General, Matthew Hopkins.

Hopkins was born in 1620 at Great Wenham, Suffolk to James Hopkins who was a puritan preacher. Much of Matthew's early life is a mystery but he starts to appear in the historical record around 1644 following the trial of a coven of witches in the Essex town of Manningtree where he was living at the time.

In his book *The Discovery of Witches*, published in 1647, he answers some of the many questions that were proposed to him during his time as Witchfinder General. Indeed the book itself is subtitled 'Answer to severall queries, lately' and reads as a document of questions and answers. In his book Hopkins describes one his first cases, the aforementioned case of a coven of witches from Manningtree, after a member of the public enquired about Hopkins experience in finding witches and why he happens to be so qualified in placing them on trial. Hopkins answered:

The Discoverer [Hopkins himself] never travelled far for it, but in March 1644 he had some seven or eight of that horrible sect of Witches living in the Towne where he lived, a Towne in Essex called Maningtree, with divers other adjacent Witches of other towns, who every six weeks in the night (being always on the Friday night) had their meeting close by his house and had their severall solemne sacrifices there offered to the Devill, one of which this discoverer heard speaking to her Imps one night, and bid them goe to another Witch, who was thereupon apprehended, and searched, by women who had for many yeares knowne the Devills marks, and found to have three teats about her, which honest women have not: so upon command from the Justice they were to keep her from sleep two or three nights, expecting in that time to see her familiars, which the fourth night she called in by their severall names, and told them what shapes, a quarter of an houre before they came in, there being ten of us in the roome, the first she called was

1. Holt, who came in like a white kitling.

2. Jarmara, who came in like a fat Spaniel without any legs at all, she said she kept him fat, for she clapt her hand on her belly and said he suckt good blood from her body.

3. Vinegar Tom, who was like a long-legg'd Greyhound, with an head like an Oxe, with a long taile and broad eyes, who when this discoverer spoke to, and bade him goe to the place provided for him and his Angels, immediately transformed himselfe into the shape of a child of foure yeeres old without a head, and gave halfe a dozen turnes about the house, and vanished at the doore.

4. Sack and Sugar, like a black Rabbet.

5. Newes, like a Polcat. All these vanished away in a little time. Immediately after this Witch confessed severall other Witches, from whom she had her Imps, and named to divers women where their marks were, the number of their Marks, and Imps, and Imps names, as Elemanzer, Pyewacket, Peckin the Crown, Grizzel, Greedigut, &c. which no mortall could invent; and upon their searches the same Markes were found, the same number, and in the same place, and the like confessions from them of the same Imps, (though they knew not that we were told before) and so peached one another thereabouts that joyned together in the like damnable practise that in our Hundred in Essex, 29. were condemned at once, 4. brought 25. Miles to be hanged, where this Discoverer lives, for sending the Devill like a Beare to kill him in his garden, so by seeing diverse of the mens Papps, and trying wayes with hundreds of them, he gained this experience, and for ought he knowes any man else may find them as well as he and his company, if they had the same skill and experience.

You will notice from the answer that Hopkins gave that one of his methods of gaining a confession from an alleged witch was to have her constantly watched and sleep deprived for two or three days. Other tortures were also used, including making the witch walk continually for the time she was kept awake while a confession was being extracted. There is reference to these poor women suffering horrendous blisters due to this method of torture. In today's world we look upon the times of the witch trials, and it amazes us that our ancestors were such fanatics about witches and their apprehension and eventual execution, but even at the time people were questioning the methods being used. When subjected to extreme torture it is not surprising that people will confess to a multitude of things, even when not guilty of them!

The witches of Manningtree naming their imps. From Matthews Hopkins' 1647 book *The Discovery of Witches*.

What became of Matthew Hopkins? Even this there is some question about. In 1647 his burial is recorded in the parish records but his actual death remains something of a mystery. There is a seventeenth-century poem called the 'Hudibras' written by Samuel Butler (1612–1680), which leads us to believe that Hopkins may have become a victim of one his own torture routines for finding witches. The poem records that he was subjected to a swimming test. The swimming test allowed the witchfinder to discover if a person was guilty because the water would reject the body of the person in league with the devil and make her float. If she floated she was a witch! Hopkins allegedly failed this test himself and was hung for witchcraft, although there is no evidence, apart from the satirical poem, for this as a cause of death. Regardless of what finally took Matthew to his grave, he left an indelible mark on the world that is still talked about today.

Because of his brutality, it is of no surprise that many venues in Essex claim to be haunted by the restless wraith of Hopkins and his victims. The River Stour is said to bear witness to the painful screams of those tortured by Hopkins. Seafield Bay is still allegedly haunted by the ghost of Elizabeth Clarke, a woman accused of being a witch who fell under the painful gaze of Hopkins. The Witchfinder

General himself in said to haunt Mistley Place, The Red Lion and White Hart Inn in Manningtree, Hopping Bridge and the Mistley Thorn Hotel. It seems that this ghastly spook has not found rest. But then again, perhaps he has been rejected from where he should have gone due to the nature of his persecutions and cruelty.

Mersea Island Causeway,
Mersea Island

The island of Mersea is completely cut off from the UK mainland and accessible by only one causeway known as the Strood. Mersea exhibits a rich tapestry of history; pre-Roman occupation at the site is evident as well as later periods of history. Near to the causeway there lays a Romano–British round barrow, a burial mound dating between the first and fifth centuries AD, and the ghost that has been witnessed haunting the causeway has been associated with the burial at the mound hundreds of years ago. The apparition of a Roman legionary has also been witnessed walking the Strood, sometimes as a full-bodied apparition and sometimes as a partial apparition. Although a burial in the mound was discovered during excavations there – cremated human remains were found sealed in an urn – there is no proof that the discovery is connected to the phantom Roman soldier who still appears late at night on the causeway.

Moot Hall, Maldon

The Moot Hall in Maldon was originally built in the fifteenth century for the D'Arcy family by Sir Robert D'Arcy, who was a royal official in the county of Essex and also an MP for Maldon in 1423. This building has been the centre of local government since 1576 when it was bought for £55 by the Corporation of Maldon. During this time the hall was also used as the town's court, which was situated on the first floor, and many people's fates would have been decided here. The building has also had other uses throughout its time. It was as a police station during the period 1839–1914, and was even equipped with cells and an exercise yard.

With such a history it is not surprising that people today report ghostly goings-on. Activity that has been witnessed here includes doors slamming by themselves, loud bangs from inside empty rooms, dark figures appearing and even furniture being moved by unseen hands!

Recently, paranormal investigators have been visiting this historic location to find out for themselves what is going on here and to attempt to record the activity, apparently with some success.

Old Tilbury Fire Station, Tilbury

Firefighters are renowned for their bravery. Rushing headlong into burning buildings and saving lives is something that is part and parcel of the work of a firefighter. So it comes as a shock to encounter one of these brave souls who refuse to enter their former workplace, the old Tilbury fire station, on their own due to the fear of a paranormal encounter!

Being in the fire service is obviously a job that requires an immense amount of commitment, dedication, energy and enthusiasm; could it be some of these elements that have led to the station becoming haunted in the first place? Who or what wanders the corridors of the fire station, for when people turn to discover who has just passed them, no one is present. Could it be the wraith of a long-dead fireman?

There have been at least two deaths recorded on the site. One of these was a woman who collapsed outside the station and was brought inside, where she suddenly died. The second death was that of a chief of the station in the 1960s. It is suggested that following the deaths of two crew members under his supervision, the chief felt that the loss of the crew were due to him. Unable to cope with his guilt, he hanged himself from a loft hatch inside the station. Could the phantom stranger in the corridors be attributable to one these poor souls?

Palace Theatre, Westcliff-On-Sea

A night at the theatre is a night of entertainment, fun and song, but sometimes you might just get more than you expect! Southend's last remaining old theatres have a reputation for ghostly goings-on, as reported by staff and performers alike.

The Palace Theatre in Westcliff-On-Sea is a grand Edwardian building, built in 1912, and is one of two theatres that today serve the local area. The other is the Cliffs Pavilion, which is the larger of the two and sits on the site of a Second World War anti-aircraft battery. But it is the Palace that has the longer history and more stories of ghosts according to the staff and the performers.

The venue was originally called the Palace of Varieties, but changed after a time to the New Palace. This building was, in its time, a very modern design of theatre. It was claimed that a clear and uninterrupted view of the stage was possible no matter where you sat. It originally seated 1,500, but today seats only 600. The building has an impressive façade compared to the bland, modern buildings that surround it.

The Palace Theatre has had a turbulent history, mainly caused by financial problems, and has changed hands many times since its opening on Monday 21 October 1912. However, it has also enjoyed periods of great shows and packed nights of entertainment. It is thought that it is this varied history that has caused some of the past visitors and owners to this grand building to return even after their deaths.

Its seems there are very few people who work there who haven't heard the ghost stories and many have even experienced something odd themselves. Footsteps are heard in empty areas and there have been reports of the strong smell of Old Holborn hand-rolled cigarettes coming from the fly floor and stage right. There have been several sightings of this ghost, thought to be that of a former Theatre Manager named 'George', who hung himself from the fly floor due to financial difficulties soon after the theatre opened in 1912. There are reports of the sound of

The Palace Theatre has a host of phantom occurrences, including footsteps and the smell of hand-rolled cigarette tobacco.

a ghostly piano being played from an empty pit, and staff also claim seats appear to be occupied by an unseen presence, usually during rehearsals!

Whether you're hoping for a fantastic night's entertainment or to see a spook, the Palace Theatre is a great night out!

Priory Park, Southend-On-Sea

At the end of one of the main routes into Southend-On-Sea there is a public park that has been used and enjoyed by the public since 1921. The park offers locals and visitors a peaceful area to escape the busy town.

Priory Park is named after the Cluniac priory that once stood in its grounds, founded by Robert Fitzsuen in the early twelfth century. Fitzsuen was a major landowner in Essex at this time and gave lands in Prittlewell to the monks of St Pancras in order to build a monastery. the Prittlewell priory became the largest Cluny priory in Essex.

The Prittlewell priory was successful and continued its work up until the Reformation when it was closed in 1536, By this time it was the richest of all the Essex monasteries. The king then sold the land to private interests and there it stayed until 1917 when it was bought by local business man Robert Arthur Jones. He, in a kindly act, gave it to the people of Southend for use as a museum. It opened in 1922 and was in fact the town's first public museum.

Only the Refectory remains today, dating back some 900 years with a nineteenth-century brick building added on by the private owners. All of the other monastic buildings have gone without trace. The site was once the heart of the local area in its time as a priory. In fact, Southend gets its name as it was situated at the 'south ende' of the priory's land. In the priory's heyday, Southend consisted of nothing more than a few fishing huts – a far cry from today's bustling seafront town.

Today the park is a much enjoyed by locals. It has ancient fishing ponds, a children's play area, tennis courts, peaceful walled gardens and a museum as well as large, open green areas perfect for picnics or just lazing a summer day away! The park also has an ancient brook running through it in which certain artefacts have been found which indicate that humans have settled by this brook since at least the Bronze Age. The park also has annual concerts put on by the local council, much loved by the locals and visitors alike.

But the park seems to have a dark, spooky side too. Many reports by locals seem to give strength to the idea that Priory Park in Southend-On-Sea is indeed haunted!

The history of the area lends itself to the idea that ghosts may still haunt the area, spanning several millennia with many ups and downs, and it of course has the obligatory stories of ghost monks and white ladies.

My own venture into the world of the paranormal started with an experience in this very park. While visiting the priory just before closing time. I and a friend witnessed things so strange that to this day, even with extensive research and rational thinking, I cannot explain exactly what happened. We both approached the window at the rear of the building and heard chimes. This was nothing weird in itself. We then turned left towards a large stone wall. We looked over the wall and saw the fountains and walled gardens and thought we would go sit by them for a while before we left. At the same time we both noticed how dark it had got, and how quiet things were. There is a major dual carriageway nearby, one of the main routes into Southend, and at the time we thought it was weird that we couldn't hear any traffic. However, we put these thoughts aside and continued to walk alongside the wall to try and get to the fountains. We had to follow the wall until it took us all the way to the front of the buildings. What we found when we got to where we had started shocked us. The wall we had followed round now wasn't there. After around 20 feet it stopped, in ruins. Both of us were very freaked out, to put it mildly. We knew we had followed the wall all the way around the priory but now, minutes later, it was gone! Both of us then spent the night trying to explain what had happened, to retrace our steps to work out if we had been mistaken somehow, but we knew that we remembered them from only five minutes beforehand!

To this day we have no exacting explanation of what could have happened. One possibility is that we had experienced is what is known as a time slip. This is where an area somehow slips back in time, meaning that what we saw was the area as it was in times past, with walls as they were when they were in their original state. These theories will stay just that, as there is no way to test such a hypothesis! Whatever happened, it certainly sparked my interest for the unknown and my thirst to learn more!

When researching the park and its ghost stories we found there were many more stories of people experiencing what they perceive to be ghosts. Many of the accounts come from people fishing at night. During research I spoke to Ben Street, a friend and work colleague, who regularly fishes at night at the park's large pond. He have told me of many who people believe they have seen ghosts there, or have felt that they are being intensely watched by unseen eyes, Some of the night anglers' sightings are of a female in white. She seems to be the most regular ghost, usually seen by the water's edge. Some say she seems sad, as if she has lost something dear to her.

Others are sure they have seen monk-like figures in the grounds at night, near to where the original priory would have stood. Could this be the stone theory at play? It is thought that some materials, particularly some types of rock and stone, can absorb certain types of energy, such as light and magnetism, and that in some conditions the energy is released or replayed. This type of ghost is said to never react to people, as it is not a spirit of the dead but just a playback of times past. Monks are a common sighting for this type of ghost. It is thought that as monks did the same thing at the same time every day for hundreds of years their energy built up over time.

By day the park has a welcoming atmosphere and offers a relaxing open area away from the hustle and bustle of the town centre, but by night it can take on a different atmosphere altogether, especially around the priory grounds, and these stories of ghosts will continue.

Purdeys Estate, Rochford

Purdeys industrial estate lies just to the east of Southend airport, not far from the historic town of Rochford. Until recently, when I was asked to research the location, I had no idea of the history of the site. The estate is situated near some historic landmarks, such as the aforementioned Southend airport, which in the Battle of Britain was a fighter base and saw its fair share of loss of life and injury. it is also just a stone's throw away from Rochford Hall, once occupied by Mary Boleyn, sister of Henry VIII's second wife, Anne. While the area certainly has a fascinating history to it, Purdeys itself is a modern industrial estate that belies the history that was once played out nearby.

This unassuming location came to my attention when I was working as a mobile phone engineer and a colleague, Niki, who knew about my interests in the paranormal, told me of her experiences at one of her past jobs. Niki also has an interest in the topic and she was happy to relate her story to me.

Niki worked at a warehouse in Fleet Hall Road on the Purdeys estate, for a company that repairs shoes. At first the job was like any other, but that was soon to change with the fascinating and somewhat scary events that she and others experienced.

After a short while working there she started to feel that all was not what it should be. In parts of the building, she said, she sensed that the atmosphere was different, Niki recounted that it was hard to explain exactly what she felt, just that something felt wrong. For example, one area in particular sometimes came across as dirty, as if the air was thick with something. It would be so strong on occasions that she would use her sleeves as a makeshift face mask. But she could see no reason for this phenomenon. It was more than just a damp or musty smell; she also experienced oppressive feelings at the same time, and she certainly didn't like being in there for too long.

In another part of the warehouse, situated at the back of the building, both Niki and a work friend, on more than one occasion, saw shapes and figures apparently walking through the storage shelves. Niki herself could only see shadows but her friend says she saw people! They would just walk through the storage shelves as if they weren't there. As if this wasn't unsettling enough, Niki began to notice other odd smells, including cigar smoke, an earthy, muddy smell, toffee and, disturbingly, stale blood – she could identify no source for any of these aromas!

The activity seemed to step up a notch when Niki was working one Sunday. She remembers that one of the side doors were open and the wind coming in caused some cardboard boxes to flap about, making some noise. Niki says she then heard voices. She could hear two men talking hurriedly and a third moaning as if in pain. One of the disembodied voices came across as if he was panicking, while the other seemed calmer. At first Niki thought it was customers talking among themselves, but she was soon to learn that no-one was there. The voices continued. She recounts how one of the men's voice was shouting at the other, as if telling him what to do. When she approached the area where the voices where emanating from she saw nothing but sensed the earthy and bloody odours that she had smelt before. Interestingly her friend said she saw a soldier standing by the counter, not long after Niki had heard the ghostly voices. The friend stated that the soldier was standing very straight and looking directly at her before simply vanishing.

Probably the strangest thing to have happened during Niki's time at the company was to a man called Andy. He was a very quiet man who kept himself to himself. He did his job and was a pleasant enough person, he was just rather shy and he very rarely spoke to anyone. One day, Niki came down from the office to find all the warehouse staff surrounding poor Andy, who was shaking and very pale. He was looking people in the eye and pointing to the top of the warehouse. Then he rushed upstairs to the Managing Director to ask if he could check the cameras. Andy said that something had come towards him, and gone straight through him; he described it as a big, dark shadow. Everyone could see that he was genuinely frightened and for Andy to put himself at the centre of such attention speaks volumes.

Niki herself believes that the site is so impregnated with the energy of emotional and traumatic events of the past that an imprint has been on the area which replays the events for all to see and hear. These events, when replayed, are chilling snippets of the history of the building that used to occupy the site.

I was approached by Niki and asked to help to find out more about this location that could possibly explain all, or maybe even some of, the phenomenon that many people have experienced in this modern industrial building. My first step was to find out what was previously on the land, so I crossed-referenced maps from today and past maps of the area. One discovery seemed to fit with the reported activity. I found that as early as 1922 there was an infectious disease hospital located exactly where the new shoe repair building is today on Fleet Hall Road. On further research, we discovered that the hospital was used during the Second World War to treat injured pilots and ground crew as it was only a short distance away from RAF Rochford, a frontline fighter base heavily involved in the Battle of Britain. The airfield and the surrounding area was attacked on many occasions causing injury and loss of life. In fact Southend was a military town during the war, with most people being evacuated as the military moved in. Many areas of Southend were bombed during the war years including the high street and the nearby radar station at Canewdon. A V2 rocket even hit the area that is now Adventure Island! This would certainly help explain why military men have been seen in the building. The employees' hearing men in pain would also be explained by the fact that the hospital cared for those contaminated with infectious diseases and horrific injuries sustained in the process of war. Several of these hospitals were built in the area. The walls of one in Westcliff-On-Sea can still be seen today although nothing else remains as new housing was built on the site.

One can hardly be surprised that many in the area today have heard or felt anything that shouldn't be there; with modern medicines at our disposal, it is hard for us to imagine just how much suffering the afflicted patients went through. Men of medicine would help as much as they could but until the advent of modern antibiotics there was not a lot they could do to help except try and ease the suffering. It is no wonder the energy of these people is thought to have been imprinted into the area and cause the activity that has been witnessed over the years.

This area of Purdeys industrial estate overlays the site of the former Fleet Hall Road infectious disease hospital.

Red Lion Hotel, Colchester

When it comes to haunted buildings, usually everyone hopes to hear tales of murderous deeds, tragic accidental death, gore, frightening supernatural events and maybe even a sex scandal thrown in for some good measure. If you want to hunt for ghosts in such a location, then look no further than the Red Lion Hotel in Colchester, for it shall not disappoint.

The hotel is a Grade I listed building and according to the website of Brook Hotels, the company that currently owns the property, it is 'a fine example of Tudor England'. One cannot deny the beauty of this building, and its history is as fascinating as it is remarkable.

The most famous of the Red Lion Hotel's ghostly residents is that of Alice Miller. It is claimed that in 1633 Alice's throat was slashed at the hotel. The reason for her murder, or even suicide, which possibility shouldn't be discounted, is her discovery that she was pregnant. Some stories say that Alice was having an affair with a well-to-do gentleman. On discovering the news of pregnancy, her lover, who could not be involved with her due to class differences, or he may have even been married, lured Alice to the hotel where he murdered the luckless girl and their unborn child.

The other possibility, bringing another twist to this tale, is that the father to Alice's child was none other than her own father. It is here where the story diverges: either Alice took her own life, or her father murdered her, not wanting to be discovered to be the father of his own daughter's child.

You may be thinking that it seems to be a clear-cut murder. After all, who on earth could manage to slit their own throat? Well, it has happened before. In my previous book *Paranormal Hampshire* I covered the story of an actor at the New Theatre Royal in Portsmouth who somehow took his own life by cutting his throat! Regardless of whether it was murder or suicide, it must have been an awful way to die.

The Red Lion Hotel.

The bar area of the Red Lion Inn looking towards the Parliament Restaurant. This is the place where the wraith of poor Alice Miller has been witnessed most frequently. Photograph © Steve Moyle

Alice is not the only ghost said to haunt the hotel though. Witnesses report seeing a woman wearing Edwardian costume, and there is also at least one account of the ghost of a gentleman dressed in cavalier clothing. One hotel guest, while resting in the lounge, claims to have seen him walk straight through a closed door and then through one of the hotels windows.

So far we have encountered incest, a gruesome murder and eye witness accounts of two ghosts. You may remember that at the start of this story I also mentioned a tragic accident, and no accident can be more tragic than the one I now recount.

In the 1970s a group of monks brought some children on a trip and stayed at the hotel. A sudden fire broke out close to their rooms. Although many of the guests made it to safety, it is said that at least one monk and several of the children died in the inferno. Since that time, guests staying at the hotel have complained about the sounds of panicking children running about the corridors. It is so sad to think that people died so young and in such horrific circumstances, and may still be reliving their tragic ordeal.

Other supernatural experiences to be had at the hotel include doors opening and closing even when they are apparently locked, objects moving of their accord,

Room 10 at the Red Lion Hotel. It is here that guests complain of the sounds of the panicking children who perished in a fire at the hotel in the 1970s. Photograph © Steve Moyle

inexplicable noises, sudden cold spots, sensations of being watched by unseen eyes and lights swinging on their own. Such happenings all serve to complement the ghost sightings to be had at this historic hotel.

In the course of my research I was lucky enough to discover that the hotel has recently undergone some paranormal investigations, in January 2012, under the directorship of Steve Moyle from Ghost Hunt Events (www.ghosthuntevents.co.uk)

When I asked Steve for his impressions on the hotel he told me 'Ever since this venue had been booked for a ghost hunt my team and I were anxious to investigate this amazing location, a building that has plenty of history and known ghosts, and the very fact that just about every room that we were staying in had some interesting history, usually macabre.' As well as being director of Ghost Hunt Events, a very reputable company exploring the paranormal, Steve is also a Spiritualist medium. This ability no doubt gives him an extra edge when investigating the ghosts here. I was very interested in hearing about what the team experienced during their time at the Red Lion and Steve happily brought me up to speed on the spooky happenings he and his team encountered.

Soon after arriving we split into two teams. After a while I suggested that we hold a séance to try to get spirit to come forward and give the group some form of personal evidence.

After a short amount of time a young boy called Timothy aged about six or seven years. The group had already detected him via the tricorder and our other electronic equipment. Timothy was wearing a smart suit with short trousers, not a school uniform, and by his appearance he looked as if he came from the 1810s. He also brought his sister, called Mary, with him but she was rather shy. However between them they managed to move the arms of some of the guests. Hot and cold spots were also felt by the guests, but generally the energy seemed only to interact with those nearest to the kitchen.

There was also another female energy present, she was about twenty-three years old and was very shy. She emerged from the kitchen area and stayed within an invisible boundary from the kitchen door to mid-way into the restaurant. She did not interact with the guests, but she could see that Timothy and Mary were interacting with us.

Throughout the séance I could sense a male energy sitting near the bar. He seemed to be very grumpy, almost angry, and he appeared to be dressed in clothing which I would associate with being from 1920s or 1930s. He did not want to interact with the group and stayed in the same place, muttering to himself.

After we broke the séance circle I conducted an EVP (Electronic Voice Phenomena) experiment, which was stopped mid-flow due to a very noisy crowd making their way along the walkway just outside, but after we re-commenced the experiment there were two EVPs recorded. One has been added to our website as it is very clear; in the other we cannot establish what exactly is being said.

You can listen to the clear one at http://youtu.be/XnZ-HpNAgvM.

It seems that positive results happened for the team at Ghost Hunt Events quite quickly, so I decided to press Steve for what he thought was the most active area of the entire hotel and where he feels they experienced the most noteworthy evidence. Steve told me

The cellar, which is situated on the other side of the public walkway. This was a very spooky place and the group was split. The majority of us were in the main cellar and a couple of guests were near to the beer cask entrance, where the other group reported some strangeness when they were here.

A male energy joined us. He was from Norfolk, aged between seventeen and nineteen years old, called Phillip and seemed to be a very simple-minded chap. He did not physically interact with the group. Instead, we heard all manner of strange noises like groaning, whistling, loud bangs, knocking and all-round weird noises.

Part of the cellar where the paranormal investigators from Ghost Hunt Events experienced all manner of inexplicable knocks, bangs, raps and taps. Photograph © Steve Moyle

Every time something happened all of the guests jumped, as these noises came with no warning. They were not caused from people walking on the pavement outside, as we could hear everything that was happening on the street above; the noises in the cellar were coming from the floor or from within the hotel.

The group of people who stayed by the beer cask entrance heard and felt much more than they bargained for; on many occasions some very loud bangs and crashes were heard in this area and just after the noises the guests who were near that area screamed!

Already it appears that the Red Lion Inn maybe willing to give up some of its paranormal secrets, and with more future investigations planned, what evidence will be discovered in the years to come?

Rochford Hall, Rochford

This historic house was once rumoured to have been the birthplace of the beheaded queen, Anne Boleyn. Although those rumours have now been dismissed, it is certain that Anne Boleyn would have spent time at Rochford Hall; indeed her father Thomas (1477–1539) owned the property. A replica stained glass window displaying the heraldic coat of arms of Queen Anne can still be seen. There are suggestions that Anne actually met King Henry VIII for the first at the hall and this is the place where their romance blossomed. I wonder if Anne would have associated herself with the king had she known that she would succumb to the executioner's axe at the Tower of London in 1536 after only three years of marriage!

The ghost of Anne Boleyn has been reported in numerous places including the Tower of London, Blickling Hall in Norfolk, Hever Castle in Kent and the Tudor Merchants' House in Southampton. Perhaps Rochford Hall can also join the list of places that she haunts, as it is said the headless apparition that has been witnessed at the hall must be that of Anne. It is also worth noting that the ghost's appearances can be somewhat different. Some of those that have witnessed the ghost have claimed it is headless, while others state seeing nothing more than the humanoid shape of what they believe to be a woman. Regardless, it appears that Rochford Hall may well be an interesting place for ghost hunters of the future to investigate. For now, the hall is a private residence and therefore the owners' privacy must be respected.

Saffron Walden, Uttlesford

The picturesque village of Saffron Walden is steeped in history and many of the medieval buildings that still grace the streets, hundreds of years since they were built, and many of the old buildings have ghosts stories attached to them. But the story we discuss here concerns a ghost from a more recent period in history.

During World War Two, two airfields were constructed near Saffron Walden, these being Debden and Little Walden. Both of these bases were heavily active during the Battle of Britain and then in the later stages of the war during the bombing campaigns against Germany. There was a high casualty rate among aircrews. Some never returned, and those who barely scraped back in their damaged planes were often badly injured. The control towers would have been hives of activity and emotion, especially when crews were expected back. Imagine the tense waiting until the planes, some limping and with engines smoking, finally appeared over the horizon. It is no wonder that these airfields seem to have energy to them and have so many sightings of airmen decades after the war finished. Many of the once bustling airfields have been silent for over half a century and many of them returned to farmland use.

Saffron Walden is no exception to this. One story of a ghostly United States Army airman says that on the fiftieth anniversary of his demise his ghost was seen sitting on the backseat of a car that was passing the site of the crash. Was he possibly trying to get a lift back to the airfield, not realising he had died? Some witnesses have said that they hear the sounds of activity on what would have been the airfield to this day.

Southend Pier, Southend-On-Sea

Southend's famous pier has entertained many millions during its long lifetime and has seen a fair amount of ups and downs, from its heyday when it thronged with day trippers, to the string of accidents including boat crashes and fires that have plagued its history. The pier started life as a small, wooden construction, its original purpose being to make it easier for people to get to Southend. Early tourists were dropped off by boat since the road networks were not yet equipped to cope with the increasing number of visitors to the area. It became one of the main attractions in Southend for day trippers from London; thousands were entertained by the theatres and amusements at the end of the pier. The grand old structure also served its country during both World Wars and survived unscathed.

The area around Southend's seafront has many stories of ghosts. Some of the town's older pubs such as the Minerva and the Hope Hotel, both eighteenth-century buildings, have seen many events. Fun drunken nights, drunken fights and even murder have all been witnessed by these old buildings, so it is no surprise that ghost stories are prevalent in this area. The pier, it seems, is no exception. One recent case is quite interesting.

Not so long ago the pier entrance was given a facelift, along with much of Southend High Street. The new renovations, styled in modern glass and metal, gave the seafront a much needed makeover. However during the building work, construction workers reported some strange things. One builder ran away in fright at the sight of a ghost in 'old-style clothes'! He was stopped by police as he fled the scene. The officer seemed convinced by the builder's account of the sighting. Maybe the disturbance of the area caused a ghost to make its appearance? Recent research has shown that during the early stages of the renovation of the pier entrance, cellars and underground toilets, presumably of buildings that served the pier in times past, were found. These buildings were a complete surprise to the local council; they had no knowledge of any buildings being there, or of the sewers and other

The pier at Southend-on-Sea.

The head of Southend Pier can be seen in the background.

The entrance to the pier.

infrastructure found by the builders. It is well-known that during construction work or the refurbishment of old buildings many report seeing, feeling and hearing ghosts, and some actually experience significant paranormal activity during the renovation process.

As far as we know, no more sightings from that area have been reported since...

St James the Less, Hadleigh

The church of St James the Less in Hadleigh is rumoured to be haunted by a particularly colourful character, James 'Cunning' Murrell.

Mr Murrell was known as a local 'cunning man' and was believed by many to have supernatural powers. It is claimed that he could cure illness, divine for lost objects, break spells and was also clairvoyant. It is also said that one night he paid a visit to a witch practicing the 'black arts' and, disgusted with her acts, commanded her to drop dead... she promptly complied! Murrell was certainly a master of many divine trades. His skills earning him the title 'Master of Witches'. Perhaps the most amazing of his abilities, which I came across while researching this story, was the fact that James Murrell accurately prophesised his own death on 16 December 1860.

James Murrell is buried at St James the Less, but alas he is in an unmarked grave as he was not a Christian and was also a pauper, therefore we only know that he is buried on the north side of the church.

St James the Less church in Hadleigh, the burial site of James 'Cunning' Murrell.

A view towards the church of St James the Less from where John 'Cunning' Murrell's cottage once stood.

St Nicholas's Church, Canewdon

Canewdon church is one of the haunted centres of Essex; few other locations have as many myths and legends attached to them. From apparitions in the church to witchcraft myths, including the witch buried at the crossroads, people in the surrounding area have grown up hearing the many stories of ghostly goings-on in and around the graveyard.

I personally grew up on the myths regarding Canewdon told by my older brother. Many of my friends heard similar tales when they were young and we in turn pass these local stories of ghosts on to the next generation. The legends, spooky stories and the myths of Canewdon are, to this very day, stronger than ever. At weekends, many young people come to the church in the hope of experiencing something supernatural. Unfortunately this has become quite an annoyance to some of the locals and sadly there have been incidents of vandalism at the church, with the windows of this historic building being broken. This type of behaviour is of course condemned by the ghost hunting community. Care and respect should be rule number one when going on a ghost hunt, be it professional or amateur.

The church itself is situated at the west end of the main road that runs through the ancient village of Canewdon in Essex. The village is no stranger to stories of ghosts and witches, due, no doubt to, the long history the village has enjoyed. The name Canewdon itself comes from the Saxon name Caningadon, which roughly translates as 'hill of the Can people'. Some suggest that Canute the Great camped at Canewdon before the Battle of Ashingdon in 1016.

The building consists of a fourteenth-century church, while the fifteenth-century tower was constructed to celebrate the victory of King Henry V at Agincourt. It stands on a hill 128 feet above the marshes leading down to the River Crouch. The oldest part of the church is the outside wall of the north aisle which contains many Roman bricks. There have been numerous Roman finds in the village and it

The West Gate of St Nicholas's church at Canewdon.

is thought that some of these building materials left by the Romans were used to construct the new church.

These local legends have now, thanks to the internet, spread worldwide. Most of the legends are centred on witchcraft. The reason for this is quite simple. It is a historic fact that witches did exist in Canewdon. The last known witch to live in Canewdon was Granny Garner who passed away in 1977, but there were many before her, stretching back hundreds of years; there is no doubt that witches existed here. One of Canewdon's famous characters who is linked with paganism is George Pickingill, or Ol' George as he was known locally. He was the local cunning man and was feared by many. According to the legends he would stop farm machinery with just his mind and would have imps harvest the fields for him when he was a farm worker in his younger days. He became known across Essex for his abilities and knowledge. He is thought to be the source of many of the myths of Canewdon.

Legend has it that while the church tower stands there will always remain six witches in Canewdon. Local folklore also has it that if you walk around it seven times on Hallowe'en you will see a witch and if you walk around it thirteen times you will become invisible. However these myths have been subject to a type of

'Chinese whisper'. There are many variations that no-one is sure what the original myth is! It is because of these tales that the church has become a place where ghost hunters and thrill seekers alike come, at night, to investigate for themselves. So much so the police now close the area during Hallowe'en, after a riot broke out in the churchyard in 1987. Among all the myths and hype surrounding the Canewdon witches, however, there does seem to be some truth about the haunting of St Nicholas's church and graveyard.

Reported sightings can be found through various sources. One of the sightings at Canewdon was in 1987, when a visitor to the village saw a lady in blue who vanished in front of her; understandably, it gave her quite a fright! Another sighting is that of a ghost of a lady who wears a bonnet but seemingly has no face. She is seen on moonless nights, walking from the west gate northwards to the river. With the rise in interest in paranormal investigations Canewdon church has received an increase in visitors looking for the unknown, and a more serious approach has been taken by a few groups in the hope of finding out what is really going on at Canewdon. Such groups bring with them the most modern in ghost hunting equipment in the hope of documenting something that may lend credence to some of the stories surrounding the village. These ghost hunters have indeed experienced some strange goings-on.

On one investigation, after a quiet start to the night, things suddenly got interesting when a team member drew attention to a light that was seen hovering above one particular gravestone. It was caught on video and seen by four people. This light could not be readily explained by anyone present. On another investigation, bright, electric-blue sparks were seen above the same gravestone. Exhaustive searches failed to find any cause. Preceding the lights, all four investigators in the group heard heavy footsteps seemingly walk towards them. No cause was ever found. Research on the gravestone in question has found nothing odd, so the mystery endures!

I myself experienced an intriguing night at the church, ending with the heavy iron gates being shaken by unseen hands. With Essex Paranormal's co-founder, Laura Mcphilimey, I was observing the church from the west car park, a small area by the west gate of the church grounds. We had decided to experiment with some dowsing rods, as after much practice and research we thought that may be of some use during certain investigations.

We had been dowsing for around half an hour and the rods seemed to be pointing at the same area whenever asked to point in the direction of any ghost or spirit. As one of us dowsed, the other would be taking notes and photographs and observing the area. When we finished, I thanked the ghost or spirit for its time and the gates that arc in front of the west door shook with some force. We took some final photographs and quickly left!

This interesting event was further investigated when we next visited the church and studied the west door and its iron gate and found it hard to re-create the sound we heard. During the original investigation we were close enough to see no-one was there. We originally went to Canewdon not expecting anything to happen as we believed the myths were just that, myths, not backed up by any facts or real evidence. Nights like this one have caused me to change my opinion of the location! While many of the reports of ghostly goings-on here might be down to people expecting too much and jumping at the slightest noise, it would seem that not all are.

Another particularly frightening event also took place in the west car park, in late 2003. Two investigators had just pulled up and were getting their equipment ready when something banged on the side of the car. As one of the investigators went to grab a camera another loud bang was heard against the driver's side door, but there was no-one to be seen outside! The bangs were quite considerable and certainly startled both investigators.

So it seems despite for all of its myth and legends, the church at Canewdon does indeed to have some strange goings-on. Maybe we will never know exactly what or who is causing such activity and the mystery continues...

St Nicholas's Church.

St Osyth Priory, St Osyth

The village of St Osyth lies between Clacton-On-Sea to the west and Colchester to the south-east. It was named after the first Anglian princess to convert to Christianity. St Osyth came to Essex after her marriage to Sighere, King of Essex, and lived here until her death around AD 700. It is said that Danish Vikings beheaded St Osyth and, in true supernatural fashion, where her body fell to the floor a spring gushed forth and St Osyth's decapitated corpse rose up, collected her own head in her arms and walked to the nearest convent where her mortal remains then collapsed to the ground.

The ghost of St Osyth, carrying her own head, has allegedly been seen in the vicinity of the well that sits on land owned by St Osyth's Priory. The well is said to be the site upon which St Osyth was beheaded. The priory itself is also said to hold a member of the ethereal realm. The ghost of a brown-clad monk has been seen here, but who he is remains unknown.

Sun Inn, Saffron Walden

The Sun Inn has a Cromwellian and Civil War history attached to it. This violent era of our history saw Englishmen kill Englishmen and family fight against family. Fear around the country was at an all time high. Today the Sun Inn is no longer a public house, but the building remains and now houses other businesses. People have reported seeing a Cromwellian soldier in the older parts of the building. Furniture moves by itself and many times people have thought that someone has broken into the building because of the noises, but on closer inspection no intruders are ever found.

The Sun Inn in Saffron Walden has a very distinctive historical feeling to it and one can imagine Civil War Troops based here, drinking their cares away.

Swan Hotel, Brentwood

Being chained to the wall in the cellar of a public house is probably not your idea of the best way to spend your last night on earth, but this is exactly what happened to William Hunter. William was a Protestant who refused to be subjugated by Catholic persecution and was unwavering in his religious conviction even when faced with threats and eventually a death sentence. For a seventeen-year-old man he certainly showed commitment and dedication to his chosen faith. But that would not save him.

On 27 March 1555 William was burnt at the stake. Perhaps it is the ghost of William that has been experienced at the Swan public house in Brentwood. Staff have reported arriving for work and seeing what they believe to be customers waiting at the bar doors but when they go to let their patrons in the people have simply vanished.

The site upon which poor William was martyred is today within the grounds of Brentwood School and the exact spot of his execution is marked with an elm tree known as the Martyr's Elm.

Sandy Drawbridge is the current landlady of the Swan and she too has had some very unusual experiences while living in the private apartments at the pub.

My family members have said they have felt someone sitting on the end of their beds while they were sleeping and my sister awoke one night to witness a middle-aged lady dressed in an old-fashioned nightgown peering over the top of her. The experience frightened her so much so that she slept with the light on for the next eight months. A few months back we had a team of psychics and mediums visit the pub in an attempt to find out more about the ghosts. They said that we had five ghosts here at the Swan but I am not sure how accurate that is.

Brentwood School as pictured on a postcard in 1847. The large tree to the right is the Martyr's Elm and marks the spot where William Hunter was burned at the stake in 1555.

Valentines Mansion, Ilford

Valentines Mansion is a late-seventeenth-century family home that has had a variety of uses during its lifetime including tenure as a home for refugees during the First World War, an office complex, a hospital and a health centre from the 1920s onwards.

In the mid-1990s the building was abandoned. As with any historic property that is not carefully monitored and maintained on a regular basis, time took its toll on the mansion, which descended into a state of dilapidation. It is thanks to restoration work funded by Redbridge Council and the Heritage Lottery Fund in 2007 that Valentines Mansion is still with us to this day. Valentines Mansion is currently open to the public and is well worth a visit.

Many tales of the mansion being haunted have sprung up over time. Witnesses claim to have heard phantom footfalls, experienced strange and uncomfortable atmospheres and even seen apparitions haunting the corridors of this former family home.

Despite the mansion being investigating by many paranormal investigation groups over the past few years, I am not aware of any major breakthrough in research or evidence that shows the house to be haunted for sure. I could be wrong though and if you have investigated the mansion and have evidence that you think proves the mansion to be haunted beyond doubt then please do get in touch with me via the publishers, as I would be most interested to hear from you and see the evidence you have.

While researching this piece for *Paranormal Essex*, I spoke to Georgina Green who is currently a volunteer historian at Valentines Mansion, who stated 'I can't say there are any real ghosts of Valentines, though several groups have held vigils on different evenings over the last five or so years. I did sit in on one occasion but they got nothing worth mentioning. Those of us who have been in the building late and/or alone feel it is a happy house and that if there are any ghosts, they are pleased with what we are doing there.'

I must admit speaking from a ghost's point of view I would also appreciate the fact that people who are working in the mansion in the present day are putting so much time, effort and care into the preservation of my old family home. So, if there is a possibility that the house could be inhabited by some spectral residents, does Georgina know who these souls may be or why they remain?

There was a ghost story which gained strength in the 1970s, and was thought to be true by someone who was a local policeman at that time. It was with regard to Clementina Rose Ingleby, who was born 27 December 1857 at 35 Carpenter Road, Edgbaston, which had been the family home since her parents married in 1850. However, the family returned to live at Valentines (the home of Mrs Ingleby's uncle and her childhood home) sometime in the 1860s. People claimed they had seen the ghost of Clementina. There are stories that she threw herself down the stairs, or out of the balcony window, or drowned herself in the lake. Maybe she tried to commit suicide as a teenager, but it would be difficult to find out if there is any truth in that theory, unless it got into the newspaper (which is unlikely) and someone has time to go through from about 1887 until 1894 looking for the story. I do know that in 1894 Clementina had an operation which in those days was dangerously experimental, and her mind became affected. By 1906 the family had her certified as of 'unsound mind' and she was living at Wimbledon. However, by the 1930s she was living at Church House, Heacham, Norfolk, and was referred to by a member of the family, who remembered, 'Aunt Rose was an invalid'. When she died in 1938 she was buried in the family plot at Heacham. I feel that she was more just unable to look after herself than actually a 'lunatic'.

I also spoke to someone who said she had worked in the house many years ago when it was council offices and she heard a baby crying or something like that. At the time I couldn't think of any explanation, but I have since heard a story which might explain a ghost. Apparently a lady who lived in the house in around 1921 gave birth to twin babies and smothered them – regarded at the time as a sad tragedy by a young mother who was very depressed. This was soon after the end of the Great War and the building was a temporary home for four families at that time.

Well, there is certainly a history behind the house that could herald spectral links. The sad story of a lady smothering her children is tragic enough. Throw into the mixture the possibility of Clementina Rose committing suicide at the property and you could have the foundations of a very plausible ghost story ... or a complete myth. What do you think?

Walton Hall Museum, Stanford-Le-Hope

Walton Hall Museum is a venue that has recently appeared on the spectral map for ghost hunters everywhere due to its hauntings.

The main building at the site dates from the seventeenth century but Walton Hall Museum's association with history stretches much further back, to the time of the Roman Empire's occupation of England. Despite the knowledge that Walton Hall has a far-reaching history, little else is known about the site and the current owners have not been able to discover much more about the place. Their research continues and perhaps in the future they may be able to discover something in the historical record that binds the ghosts of this museum to the place to this day.

In order to uncover more about the ghosts of Walton Hall Museum I initially contacted the owners – the first port of call for any research into the paranormal. Coral Wood deals with all the museum's paranormal investigations and ghost hunts and she was very happy to talk about the sites alleged supernatural residents.

> We opened the museum to members of the public some eighteen years ago and since that time we have had sightings of a few ghosts here. There are four ghosts here but the most commonly reported is the apparition of a small old man who has been seen wandering around the museum and our surrounding land. He has been described as being short, wearing a flat cap, an old-style shirt and a baggy trousers that are tied up with string around the waist and ankles. Who he is we don't know for sure, so can only theorise that he is perhaps a past farmer or farmhand that worked here in days gone by

The ghost of the old man gives us one ghost, so who are the ghosts of other three spooks that haunt here? 'There are also the ghosts of a woman and child and we believe they are distinctly connected to the fourth ghost' At this stage Coral informed me that much of the information concerning the fourth ghost has come from psychics and mediums. These talented people, in a majority of cases, can throw some interesting thoughts and theories into the ghost hunting cooking pot but obviously, until science can prove or disprove mediums for certain, all they can offer are theories (albeit allegedly coming direct from the ghosts themselves).

Coral continued, 'The fourth ghost is not a nice character at all. He doesn't like women but he does like ... how can I put it ... children, in a rather disgusting way.' The ghost of a paedophile is something I have only ever encountered once before so I was a little intrigued by how the information about this character and his disturbing mindset came about. 'Mediums and psychics have picked up on him quite a bit. He passes on graphic images to them and they think the ghosts of the woman and the child that haunt here are connected to him as well. They also say that he looks disfigured ... like he has been burnt down one side.'

Bibliography

Dening, John C., *Restless Spirits of Lagenhoe* (2000)

Downes, Wesley, *Memories of an Essex Ghost Hunter* (2009)

Green, Andrew, *Phantom Ladies* (1977)

Hallam, Jack, *Haunted Inns of England* (1972)

Jones, Richard, *Haunted Inns of Britain & Ireland* (2004)

Puttick, Betty, *Ghosts of Essex* (2007)

Scanlan, David, *Paranormal Hampshire* (2009)

Scanlan, David, *Paranormal Wiltshire* (2009)

Underwood, Peter *et al.*, *The Borley Rectory Companion* (2009)

About the author:
David Scanlan

David Scanlan's interest in the paranormal started in 1986 when his sister moved into a three-bedroom council house in the northern suburbs of Portsmouth, Hampshire. Shortly after she moved into the property all kinds of supernatural activity started. Objects were thrown around, black shadowy figures were seen flitting up and down the stairs and the spectre of a man wearing 1940s clothing witnessed standing in the back garden. It was this poltergeist-ridden house that started David on the path he now treks.

In 2001 David established the Hampshire Ghost Club. Its aims are to investigate claims of paranormal phenomena and where possible record this evidence for dissemination among the public at large. The Hampshire Ghost Club gained a good reputation quickly and still stands out as a major ghost hunting society, investigating all sorts of locations around the UK but specialising in hauntings of the county of Hampshire.

The public have seen David's work in action with numerous radio and TV appearances including Living TV's popular series *Most Haunted* and *Most Haunted Live*.

David was born in Portsmouth, Hampshire, and currently resides in the small market town of Romsey, Hampshire with his wife and four children.

About the author:
Paul Robins

Paul Robins' first foray into the world of the paranormal was at the age of eight or nine, when he organsied a ghost hunt in his junior school PE shed, which he and some friends were convinced was haunted! He also grew up hearing the local myths of ghosts and witches at locations such as Canewdon church and Hadleigh Castle, which always stirred his imagination.

It wasn't until the late 1990s that Paul had his first paranormal experience in which he and a friend saw parts of an old priory that no longer exist. This experience shook him at first, but really fuelled his interest in all things paranormal and by early 2003 he started to visit the places he was told so much about as a child, to see for himself if any of the myths were true. After a year of reading and learning as well as attending ghost hunts with a well established group he decided to start his own group with his then partner.

He and Laura Mcphilimey started Essex Paranormal in early 2004 and spent three years investigating around the country, gaining respect from the ghost hunting community and even becoming the in-house paranormal experts at the former military base of Maes Artro in Wales. Essex Paranormal has appeared in numerous local newspapers and even assisted in research for TV companies such as ITV. Paul has a background in electronics and in particular avionic systems repair, and so it was his job within the group to oversee the technical side such as the equipment used during paranormal investigations.

Paul has a great love of history, especially the First and Second World Wars with which he feels a strange affinity.

He currently lives in Southend-On-Sea with his partner and daughter.

David Scanlan, *above*, and Paul Robins, *left*

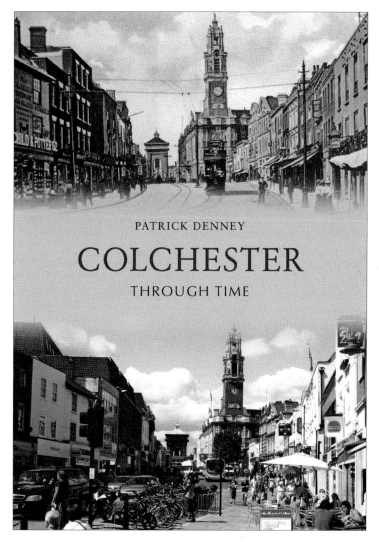

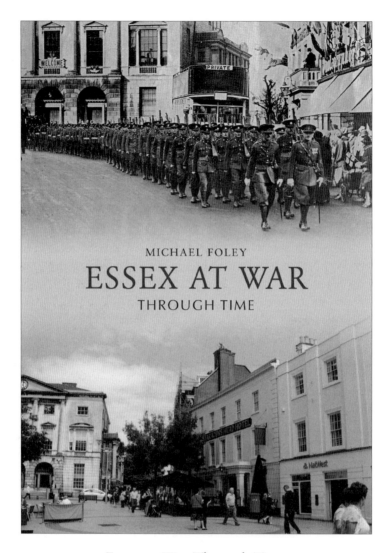

Essex at War Through Time
Michael Foley

This fascinating selection of photographs traces some of the many ways in which Essex has changed and developed over the last century.

978 1 84868 653 3
96 pages, full colour